UNLEASH YOUR POWER

UNLEASH YOUR POWER

Own your Energy, Mindset and Strengths

Kirsten Blakemore

New Edition

Edited by Sue Blakemore

ACKNOWLEDGMENTS

For me, writing a book continues to be a culmination of experiences, wisdom shared, and role models who have walked the road ahead.

I have a few very good friends I can process through painful experiences to gain meaning. But those friends are so valuable to me. Without their support, love, patience, and humor I would not have the forgiveness, strength, and resilience I have today.

Wisdom comes in different forms. Some, as a result of giving yourself fully and being able to look back with a deeper understanding of the why. I look to those who have been at the source of my pain as teachers. Through those experiences I have gained wisdom, and I stand here today with many PhDs. I have found being a mother of two has graced me with the understanding of what it means to love fully, to hurt fully, and to give over fully for the lives I have been so blessed to have in this life. But the cost of wisdom is high and is far from easy, or it wouldn't be wisdom. I am so grateful for my sons every day, and I thank them for their daily doses of wisdom.

To those with whom I have connected through painful experiences at work, thank you. Know I am richer for your friendships. Anique Mautner is one to whom I am so grateful. She has been an editor, brainstormer, and major support throughout the last decade. Without Anique's eye and compassion, this new edition would not have been born. Her book development expertise is bar none, and I value and appreciate her ability to see me through this work.

Finally, my role models are people who have demonstrated behaviors that have molded me into who I am today. Every business leader, athletic coach, parent (and more) must know the impact they will have on another human being's life. It is a huge responsibility. Two role models stand out in my life. My Father who struggled as a father, husband, and businessman. My father was a SERE school instructor (survival, evasion, resistance, and escape) in the mountains in Maine when I was young. Growing up we did not go to baseball games or museums with him; rather he would take us to the mountains, and we would "survive" the weekends in pretty dire weather. He could teach what few can, yet he could not cope with "normal" life. He drank and escaped until his life finally ended from the abuse. My father was a role model for me of what not to do. Whether he knew it or not, his life taught me so much about what I didn't want for mine. I love him and respect the lessons I learned from him.

My Mom was the rock of my home growing up. She was and is an example of never-ending grace and giving. To this day, her life is in service of others. Every rebellious stage (I think I only had one), every painful moment in my life, she was there for me. I have watched and experienced her love, patience, and forgiveness all of my life. For this reason, I dedicate this book to her. Without her (English teacher experience and grammar) support and her ability to make me feel like "writing a book is no big deal, just do it" I would not have the book I do today. Mom, I love you with all of my heart, and I thank you.

CONTENTS

PREFACE

I wrote the original version of this book for women: women with stalled careers who had suffered discrimination, exclusion, and less pay than men, to name a few of the negative experiences. This was a solutions book *for women* meant to support and empower them to show up as their best selves and achieve what was most important in their lives. My advocacy for women having a voice and equal rights will never waver.

What has expanded over the last several years is my perspective, having witnessed mouth-dropping moments of *people of all genders* suffering due to discrimination, gaslighting, and unfair career limitations. It became clear a revision to this book was needed to make it more inclusive of these experiences.

Bias and discrimination are still present in the workplace and the world. Perhaps they always will be. What can change is how we handle bias and discrimination.

My vision is this revised book helps people who feel held back in their careers, who have perhaps lost their way or their heart, to live in congruence with their highest values, integrity, and hopes. I offer it as a road map leading to a more fulfilling career and life through increased energy, self-awareness, and self-love.

And while this book is for leaders and aspiring leaders, the ideas are as much about self-management as they are about managing others. This is because we're also human. Where we used to separate our emotions, or personal self, from our business self, the work-from-home paradigm shift has given us permission to show up at work as our full selves. We want to feel good, from mental and physical well-being to emotional and spiritual well-being. We desire a sense of belonging: to know we are not alone in our struggles; to laugh, love and sweat; to help others and feel productive; to feel content.

What many have felt is the "bad" states too often. A lack of well-being leading to burnout and overwhelm. Not feeling good enough. Alone, overworked, underpaid, and underrecognized. Not appreciated. Fearful and unsafe.

Does transforming from *feeling bad* to *feeling good* sound unattainable? Do you rely on others to lift you back up to feeling good? Or do you unconsciously self-regulate through others?

There may be—and likely is—an outside force causing your suffering: a toxic person or situation in your life. But let's assume *you* are in control of you. With that assumption, what would it look like to reframe your thinking? To change your life from *bad* to *good* begins with an internal leap of faith. A mindset that says, *I'm afraid, but I'm doing it anyway.*

INTRODUCTION

> *"Character cannot be developed in ease and quiet. Only through experience of trial and suffering can the soul be strengthened, ambition inspired, and success achieved."*
>
> —HELEN KELLER

How often do you feel you have to prove your worth—as a married person, a parent, an employee, or a friend? Defending yourself and your value every day requires so much extra energy, doesn't it? With all the factors outside your control, it's easy to feel like a victim of both people and circumstance.

Maybe you've been impacted by others' biases and tried unsuccessfully to fight them. Maybe you questioned your own worth. *I'm not smart enough,* you think. Or maybe, *I'm not old enough* (yes, age can be correlated with experience). Experienced enough. Skilled enough. Strong enough. Good enough. Maybe you feel the daily grind, working hard both at home and at work while trying to understand office politics and hidden agendas.

Does it exhaust you? Do you feel a constant pull to take a vacation? Are you burned out? Do you feel like your physical well-being is at an all-time low? While at work, do you feel at times like you're fighting a ghost? Maybe your colleagues don't appear to value your efforts, but never tell you outright?

Challenging circumstances can certainly cause stress. The real suffering comes when, over time, you begin to question your own value. Before all else, you have to believe in yourself because dwindling self-confidence limits our ability to see all the options and take appropriate action. Discrediting our value is like a spider web touching all facets of our life; it severely impacts our confidence, our self-worth, and our ability to escape the victim stranglehold.

It took me decades of experiences to learn I'm in the driver's seat of my life. After a marriage that would turn into twenty years of what felt like prison because I shrunk to keep the peace. After a position within a toxic company that didn't value me because I was a woman who didn't share their beliefs, gender, pedigree, or religion. As in my marriage, I was invisible in this very small company. My tactic at first was to be "nice." People pleasing and say what people wanted to hear, even if I broke my honesty code. But this didn't work either. And so I began to question my worth and value. I had done everything society had taught me, everything I knew as a coach, psychology major, group facilitator—and none of it had worked. None of my training prepared me for this.

It took a failed marriage, cancer diagnosis, and a public humiliation for me to show up differently than I ever had before.

That's when real change happens. It didn't happen overnight, but as painful as it was, I found the strength to face the failed marriage and cancer as well as the people who had hurt me. I found the courage to stand up for myself and for those who experienced what I have. No longer do I sit back and witness the unfair treatment of others. I champion equity because I know what it feels like to lose your voice, becoming small and invisible with every microaggression, exclusion, and ridicule. But I also know what it feels like to be free of all that. Not because it no longer exists, but because it no longer has a stronghold. This is where we find our power.

For those who have similar experiences, this book is for you. If you feel stifled and want to release your authentic self but haven't until now for fear of not being accepted and liked. It's for all of you who need new tools to navigate challenges because the old tools just don't work anymore.

Through this book, I share challenges others have faced, how they handled them, and how they could have handled things differently to achieve a better outcome. I offer tools and frameworks to use when you find yourself in less-than-desirable positions. Finally, I offer a three-step process to creating what you want in the respective areas of your life. It's a process you can use in any situation where you feel stuck, perhaps unsure what is holding you back. These steps put you back in the driver's seat of your life where you can experience fulfillment and joy again. Many of us focus on the "how." How will I reach my goals?

How will I meet the right people to assist me? When we focus on the "how," we miss essential parts of the picture: the "why" and the "what." When we get crystal clear on *what we want* and *why it's so important to us,* the "how" starts to fall into place.

The three steps to creating your desired outcome are Define, Align, Design.

STEP 1: DEFINE

Define Your Energy: Are you perpetually exhausted and feel you lack energy? If so, this is likely how others perceive you as well. Determine the energy you bring to your meetings and personal interactions. Do you want to make people feel safe and at ease; if so, bring that energy.

Define Your Mindset: Who is in charge of your life? You are the author, the director, and the main character in your life. All the other factors, experiences, and people make up your environment.

Define Your Future: Describe your goals. Define all the parts of what you want for your life—short term and long term. What will these look like, feel like, sound like?

Define Your Strengths: Owning your strengths begins by identifying them.

STEP 2: ALIGN

Wake Up Your Life: If you seek balance, this step is about carefully selecting what you want more of in your life. If you are overwhelmed and want to be content, the choices you make, from meditation to food selection to how many meetings you agree to, all add to your current state.

Align Your Mindset: What are you thinking relative to what you want? Analyze your thoughts, define them, to then assess their alignment with your goals and dreams.

Align Outside In: Look to your environment (which consists of people, situations in which you find yourself, identify what is preventing you from moving forward) as an indicator of the alignment of your goals.

Get feedback to see how your mindset is aligned with your goals.

Get feedback to see if you're reaching your goals, and if not, why?

STEP 3: DESIGN

Courage: Disappointment and perceived failures are part of the path. Learn to correct your course. Ask for what you want.

Confidence: Fake it till you make it.

Consistency: Learn tools to follow through. Build in your accountability for your outcomes.

Measure Success: Watch for evidence and celebrate the wins!

Lead from Your Authentic Self: Courageously be *you* even at the risk of not being liked or popular.

All for One: When we are our best self, we consider others. We want to help, support, mentor others so they too can be their best. There is a ripple effect that occurs. The good reaches so many people; this is how to create scaled positive change . . . one person at a time.

In this book, I introduce new ways of thinking about your energy, your mindset, and your success. At the end of each chapter are key takeaways. After you digest the information, you have the opportunity to apply it to your situation and to journal about your experiences. I offer journaling questions to help you dive deeper into the material, to help you move forward within your life, and to achieve what you want, whether that's a successful homemaker, a promotion, or becoming a CEO—whatever life you choose.

Here are the steps to follow:

Workbook at the end of each chapter:

a. Digest the information you just read.
b. Imagine possibilities.
c. Journal.
d. Continue to add to your vision board as you build more of your dream.
e. Take action.

As with any new routine, using this three-step process—Define, Align, and Design—may feel robotic or uncomfortable at first, but the more you use this process, it becomes second nature. Doing something repetitively is key to forming a habit and shifting to organic response. Find opportunities to utilize the three steps throughout your day. Give yourself permission to slip, to fail, to move forward. Then you can apply the process to anything—from very small arguments to large goals you've always wanted to accomplish. Stick with it.

I started this three-step process years ago. I have journaled habitually, specifically defining my goals: what I want, how much, when. Detail, detail, detail. Dollar amounts for projects; details about jobs I have wanted; even health challenges with which I struggled, and what I want as an outcome. Not only has that helped me clarify what I want versus want I don't want, but I have a record of how my goals have manifested, to the detail, months later. I have manifested them *all.*

Work this process, and I'm confident the process will work for you. If you're finding it hard to make this change alone, grab a friend, family member, partner, or coach to travel this new path you are creating.

Finally, I want to underscore the importance of self-awareness of our thoughts, the stories we tell ourselves, emotions, and somatic responses we have as a result. When we become aware of what is happening inside us is when we design our lives instead of living our lives by default. When we get intentional, we unleash possibility. When possibility is unleashed, we assume our personal power.

There is no better time than now for upward, positive movement. The good news is everything is within your control. It starts with your thinking. A grateful heart and mind puts you in such a loving, receiving place. Accept the beauty in you that makes you unique to this world. Leave the world brighter because of your presence. The world will benefit from you Unleashing Your Power, your true You!

DEFINE

CHAPTER 1
DEFINE YOUR ENERGY

"Life is about the management of energy, where you place your attention is where you place your energy."

—DR. JOE DISPENZA

Think back on a time you entered a room and two people who were talking freely abruptly stopped. Did you sense the energy shift, even without hearing a word they said? Perhaps nonverbal cues made your hair stand up on the back of your neck, and you intuited an argument brewing.

You knew something happened in that room, not because you heard the conversation but because you *felt the energy*. It was electric.

Maybe you've experienced the other side of this. Being privy to work information, like a downsizing, you walk into a meeting unable to disclose the news, but you feel bad. People in the room experience your energy, whether compassionate, foreboding, or guilty.

We recognize energy, even without a word being spoken. As a group facilitator, I notice when the energy in the room slumps. If that happens, I raise my energy; inevitably the energy in the room follows.

Energy attracts or repels people. It can be strong or soft. Think of people you know who capture everyone's attention. Oprah Winfrey and Tony Robbins come to mind. Once, at a doctor's office, I couldn't help notice a sign written in bold font: "WATCH THE ENERGY YOU BRING TO THE OFFICE." This is fantastic! I reacted. We are finally recognizing what many have experienced forever: Energy is real. It matters. Even if it's only recently that you can mention energy without being considered woo-woo or out there.

Why is energy important? Many reasons. Your energy invites people into your space or makes people distrust you or puts people at ease because they feel safe in your presence.

In this way, energy impacts our well-being. It is less about *time* and more about the *quality and content* of our interactions. One day, you can have a full schedule and feel energized. The next day, depleted.

As you think about your day, what gives you energy and what takes your energy? Introverted personalities often find social interactions energy depleting; while extroverted personalities, the virtual world has been difficult because they need social interaction to feel energized.

Energy also impacts how people perceive you. How effective you are as a parent, friend, businessperson tends to correlate to the energy you bring. My boys have always sensed when I am doing well, or not, before I say anything. I have sensed the energy of a trusting manager before I really knew her, and over time, she proved to be trustworthy.

One client joined a call, and I asked, "How are you?" She said good and smiled. But her energy said something very different. When I asked, "Really?" she broke into tears.

What energy do you bring to a room? What energy do you *want* to bring? How do you want people to experience you? This is having a self-focus as well as a focus on others.

Energy changes with our state of being. Our thoughts and feelings—both conscious and unconscious—direct our energy. One reason practicing meditation is a powerful way to start the day is because it clears your mind. Then you have the space to choose your thoughts, essentially choosing your energy. You can be more intentional with your energy.

Due to our fast-paced lives where it is easy to rush through the day, you may be running on low energy and not even recognize it. After days, weeks, months of this, low energy becomes a regular state of being. One day, you wonder why you're unhappy, frustrated, lacking motivation, or even angry. It's your state of awareness, your energy, that brought you to this place, whether you are aware of the process or not. The good news is you have the power to reverse this by refocusing your energy.

A client was struggling to form a strong relationship with his boss. They didn't trust each other, and they didn't know how to connect with honesty and transparency to build a stronger relationship. He told me one day his boss wasn't honest and didn't value him. I asked him if he verified that. The answer was no. He had created a narrative resulting in hurt feelings. I asked if he wanted to hang on to that story since it was clearly causing him pain. He said no. I asked if another possible story was true. This allowed him to change the narrative—and ultimately shift his energy. Energy impacts thinking. Thinking impacts energy. He has since engaged differently with his boss, which has resulted in a more trusting relationship. Once he made the choice to trust his manager and engage without his negative narrative, he was able to take steps to build a stronger relationship. His energy was different, more trusting and positive, and his boss responded to this.

It's easy to lose track of our current energy state. Perhaps you know exactly what it's like to be caught in the commotion of being a parent, an engaged partner in your relationship, and working full time. Imagine working from home, jumping from virtual video meeting to meeting, taking care of your children, maybe a pet or two, and then having to care for close relationships. Competing priorities demand your time at all hours of the day and night. The energy required to navigate this constant activity (and sometimes drama) limits your perspective to what's happening right in front of you. It's easy to fall into the trap of doing tasks the same way you always have because your perspective and energy are limited. Worse, when you should be resting, instead you're up at 3:00 a.m. perseverating about all you have to do in the morning. Does this impact your energy? You bet.

This is what it's like for so many right now. People are struggling to lead in this new way of working or at least changing an old way of working. Some find it unbelievably difficult to manage their people virtually, to really connect with them. Others feel a sense of relief or comfort working from home: a buffer to the normal barrage of draining energy they experience in a day. For those who are highly empathetic, they can take on the energy from people and feel drained (and any other emotions they may pick up from people) by the end of the day.

In business, when emotions are high and the workload is heavy with little direction or many conflicting directions at once, employees and leaders alike can experience an overwhelmed energy. Reading the energy can sometimes come in the form of having to navigate company politics. "Why are 'they' doing this?" employees might ask or "What are the hidden agendas that I need to maneuver through successfully?" The demand to uncover the quagmire of possibilities can be overwhelming. This heavy, and often *negative,* thinking depletes us, leaving little room for big-picture thinking and self-reflection.

How do you know if you are in the midst of negative, limited thinking, feeling, and as a result, energy? Here are some descriptors that may indicate being stuck:

- A pattern of waking up in the middle of the night anxiety, thinking about work
- Working in fear you're only as good as your last project and could get fired anytime
- Very reactive
- Feeling overwhelmed
- Waning confidence
- Experiencing fear-based culture
- Priorities shifting constantly
- Having to guess the world of work politics, perceiving an unhealthy level of competition

Experiencing negative thinking that spirals downward—what I call "the swirl"—causes anxiety. In this state of mind, it becomes difficult, if not impossible, to be proactive, develop self-management skills, or focus on innovation and improvement. Lacking proactive and thoughtful leadership as well as the development of your team are some of the costs paid to working in this state of negative thinking without the ability to step out and find new perspectives.

On an individual level, if you're in the swirl of negative, looping thinking, it's made worse when everyone around you—leaders and coworkers—are in the swirl too. It compounds the problem.

As a leader, being in the swirl impacts leadership ability. There's no way you can be a proactive, good leader when you yourself are stuck in the swirl—because your energy affects others, and you won't have the perspective to find solutions or help your team find solutions. Pause. Define what's wrong. Define your energy and what is causing it. What are you thinking about that is leading to the feelings you are experiencing and ultimately your energy state?

Leaders have a responsibility to ensure the job they are asking people to do is sustainable. Dealing with high levels of ambiguity is exhausting for even the most functional teams, although some thrive in this environment. Perhaps the responsibilities you are asking people to assume are too difficult, the objectives are impossible, or the culture within the organization cannot effectively support the desired results. Check in with yourself and your people. How are they handling the culture in which they work? Identifying the gaps and then creating the right team culture to execute the strategy takes time, but it can be done. To identify problems and provide potential solutions, leaders must connect with their employees frequently with curiosity and empathy.

If you find yourself in this position without a clear, proactive direction, begin brainstorming where the gaps are and how to address them effectively and expeditiously.

An executive coach can provide a trusted sounding board to identify areas you are unable to see due to the myopic nature of this state.

It's easy to miss a looping story we have fabricated in our minds that continues to cause pain. For example, you apply for a job and receive a rejection letter. It happens again and again, and the story you believe is you will never get a new job. This belief perpetuates more negative thinking, such as, "I am not good enough," which may lead to, "I won't be able to pay my bills."

We become dangerously limited in our focus by perseverating on a problem; and this limited thinking impedes our problem-solving. We get stuck in the swirl—and stay stuck without the vision to lift ourselves from the fray. You may find yourself wound up by what he-said, she-said, which moves you into a fight, flight, or freeze mode. When that intense tunnel thinking and feeling takes over, eventually it sucks the energy from you.

This is important as you consider your well-being. What is your well-being right now? Why? Do you feel energized, which can occur when you're assigned a new, exciting project or you get a promotion? In the same way, if you receive a poor performance rating and don't agree with it, you may feel defeated and exhausted, depleted of energy.

The first step in moving outside of the negative, limited thinking is awareness and understanding your thoughts, feelings, and energy levels. Naming your state, whether it's exhausted, overwhelmed, angry, or depleted, is how you begin to change your energy.

Pay attention to emotions and subsequent thoughts. Having emotions such as dread, sadness, self-doubt, or defeat are critical indicators for change. A change can come in the form of gaining a different perspective. As a parent, one way to get out of the swirl is to drop the kids off at their grandparents or close relatives and get away for a few days. At work, when you are in the midst of burnout or energy depletion, take a vacation and separate. That distance and lack of heavy responsibility can provide a new look into the situation. Finding relief from the intense burden of swirl creates space where you can actively innovate new solutions to pressing problems. Gaining distance from the situation, you begin to see the world beyond, full of new possibilities. Within this place of awareness are deep insights. This thinking can keep a person trapped in the swirl or help to gain alternative perspectives. The shift can lead to a sense of relief where you are more likely to uncover solutions previously hidden from view. This is when you can get intentional about how you want to think and feel.

REFLECTIONS

Takeaway: You define your energy through your thoughts and feelings.

By understanding your patterns of how you cope with stress, working in the swirl, you can counter the impact it has had in the past.

Practice self-reflection.

List some of your own takeaways.

JOURNAL

- Under what conditions am I overwhelmed?
- How would I describe my energy now? What about other moments of the week?
- When am I most energized?
- When am I most depleted?

CHAPTER 2
DEFINE YOUR MINDSET

"Before assuming the driver's seat, one must find it."

—SUE BLAKEMORE

Do you feel like you're in control of your life? Or do you feel buffeted by others' choices and circumstances, allowing your boss, co-workers, friends, or loved ones to direct your life? And what is control? What if your feeling of being in control was centered in your thinking? Do you feel as though you have stumbled into the life you are currently living?

The premise of this chapter is this: Define your mindset or others will define it for you. This means owning and accepting your past, creating your present, and shaping your future. Your mindset is made up of your thoughts. Your thoughts lead to your feelings, and sometimes that loop ends up being a hamster wheel (like we discussed in the last chapter.) Thoughts like: He doesn't like me (you never verified this). I will never get that promotion (you continue to think this without looking for a solution). My work is never good enough. I am never good enough (programming from a young age but never challenged it / questioned it). I am too tired to do anymore (but there is a lack of questioning where the fatigue comes from—boredom, lack of motivation, lack of fun?). These thoughts lead to correlating emotions: sad, defeated, frustrated, confused, etc.

When stepping off the hamster wheel because you are tired of feeling bad is more important than your addiction to those draining thoughts and emotions, then you can begin to think and feel differently. Your thoughts lead to feelings. Be intentional. You can make choices that impact your behaviors—what you do.

Consider for a moment: if you had the ability to create your life, how empowering would that be? Does that question recall experiences where you felt out of control? Do you feel like exclaiming, "I didn't create that!"?

If you stick with this idea that you DID create that, though, what did you (or could you) learn from the experience? Taking back control over your life requires tremendous self-reflection, which enables you to WAKE UP YOUR LIFE and make conscious choices moving forward. The power is always in the learning, the postmortem on the event or experience you had so you can take the value, the learning, and apply this learning in the future.

MINDSETS THAT GET IN THE WAY

Below are some examples of mindsets holding you back and some propelling you forward. The key is awareness of your mindset so you can be intentional with your thinking. Maybe you've created more than what I've listed below. Beautiful! The point is to be aware of what you're thinking because it drives what comes next: your feelings, which lead to actions.

1. The Controller

I work with many people in businesses who have struggled with feeling overwhelmed, burnt out, and stuck. They feel fatigued and helpless, no longer showing up as the empowered employee they once were. The thoughts plaguing them are "I can't handle this; this is too much." Or "I am exhausted and can't keep up." In this frame of mind, they continue to focus on the problems they're facing, which keeps them stuck in the negative mindset. This thinking leads to a tornadic downward spiral that decimates everything in its path.

Time and again I hear, "Those leaders (imagine a finger pointing upward) are the problem. If we could just fix them, all our problems would be solved."

This happens in personal relationships too. And sometimes it shows up as a need to control. This need to control originates from fear.

Have you ever felt the need to control someone or something because you feared what could happen if you didn't? Because if you didn't step in, the person wouldn't act the way you want them to or the situation would turn out differently than how you'd like?

Someone I know is in a relationship in which the woman is trying to change the man, exclaiming that all the problems in their marriage rest on his shoulders. If he would change, they'd be fine. However, it doesn't work like that, I told her. We have to own what we think, feel and do, 100 percent. (By the way, that doesn't mean if someone betrays your trust, you should think you own their behavior. But you do own what you think and do in that situation in response to their offensive behavior.)

In every situation, you have a choice. You may not be able to control your environment or the people around you, but you do control yourself and your thinking. How and what you think is your choice. How you respond and react in all situations is your choice, regardless of whether the top echelon of your corporation lacks good management qualities or your partner lacks communication skills. Focus on your thoughts and response. We own 100 percent of our choices at work and in our personal relationships.

Although there will always be elements in your life you can't control, you can control you. How do you choose to show up in a situation you felt was out of your control? Every choice you make defines your now and creates your future. Look at the illustration below. Where do you fall in your current situation?

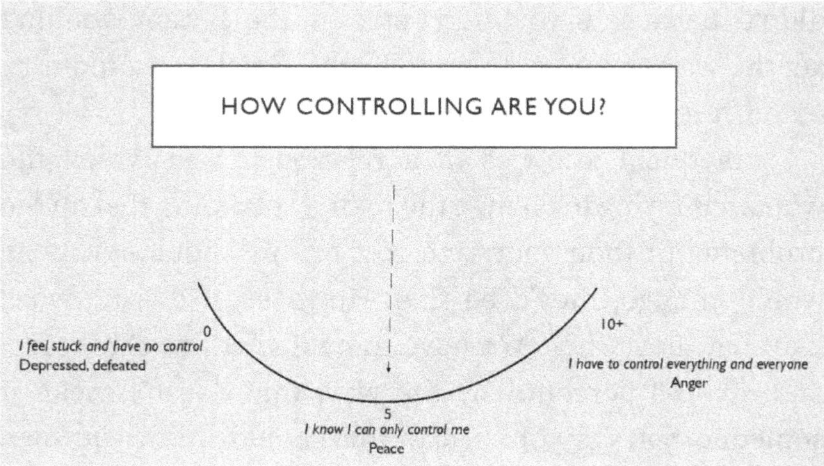

We can swing on the pendulum from where we feel stuck to where we feel so fearful of the future we try to control everything in our path. Ideally, though, we'd choose the middle where we have a sense of, "I control me, and I positively influence what's around me." This mindset offers us the greatest sense of peace.

However, if we're somewhere near either end of the pendulum arc, we'll likely feel defeated. At one end of the arc, we'd have a feeling of no control, and being stuck at the other end of the arc would make us feel very uptight and angry as we try to control everything. Sadly, when we try to control everything and everyone else but ourselves, we can't feel a sense of empowerment or peace. When we feel empowered with choice and in control of our destiny, we make space to create the future we desire, and we can be present with those we love.

2. The Inner Critic

In coaching, we name the critical voice in our heads as the inner critic, saboteur, gremlin, and so on. This inner critic we all have is so destructive if we are not aware of it. The voice that says, "I am not good enough. I am unlovable. I am fat and will never lose weight. I will never get promoted. That was the dumbest thing you said. Don't say that because they will know you are stupid." I could go on. . . .

When we are unaware of the messages the inner critic is telling us, the critic controls us via our thinking, which then causes us to respond to that thinking via emotions. When this happens, we react based on how we feel. This cycle of negative *thought–feeling–reaction* quickly turns into a hamster wheel that picks up momentum with every cycle.

Recently I worked with someone who was having intense panic attacks due to her fear of having to accomplish what felt like an impossible task. Right before making the first step in completing the arduous task, she realized her thinking was self-destructive, ineffective, and ultimately led to panic attacks. She felt incapable of taking the first step, making a phone call. To an outsider, that might sound silly—of course, she can make a call. But she was in the tornado of doubt in her mind, preventing her from completing her task. She could not see a way out. When I asked her, "You think you can't do this, correct?" She said, "Yes." "And that leads to pain?" Again, she said, "Yes." Then I asked if she were to think differently, would that redirect her feelings. She said, "Yes." The next step was to challenge her thinking—could she do this? She said, "Yes." After reflecting further, she realized her thinking had anchored her in doubt, criticism, and negative thinking, which resulted in low energy. She needed to reframe each thought. As she did this, within a short time she realized she was creating her mindset and could choose to opt out of that negative loop. The next morning, she made the first steps (including the call), which she had been unable to do for months.

Being mindful of the inner critic requires us to become aware of our limiting thinking and the messages it's sending. Some find it useful to use their emotions as indicators to tell them it's time to inspect their thinking, as opposed to the other way around. When I feel sad, I get curious about what thoughts I have making me feel that emotion.

If the inner critic is speaking to one of your core issues (like *I am not good enough, I am stupid, they won't like me*) or it is causing heavy emotion, I find it helpful to speak it out loud. I did this exercise with my son who had intense fear about driving after he had an accident. I asked him what he was thinking. When he expressed he thought he was not a safe driver, I asked him if he followed the laws. He said yes, very much so. Then I asked, what else? He said he didn't have enough experience. I asked what he thought was enough. He smiled; he knew his inner critic was telling him stories.

I asked him what story he would prefer to tell himself so he could gain confidence behind the wheel. He went on to describe his new story: I follow the rules of the road. I am a safe driver. I am aware of those around me. That made him feel better when he got behind the wheel. He has been driving with confidence ever since.

The stories we tell ourselves are powerful. Without clear awareness of our mindset, fear directs our lives. We succumb to default rather than our own design.

3. The Self-Doubter

Where this differs from the inner critic is when you believe it so much that you sabotage yourself, often unconsciously. If your inner critic has been telling you all of your life (or a good portion of it), "It will never work," "You aren't good enough," or some version of that, you will likely find ways to reinforce that. You may even create a scenario that reinforces this belief, as if to say, "See, I told you I am not good enough." To overcome unconscious self-sabotage is to admit this deep-rooted thinking is wrong. And many have a hard time with that. They would much rather be right. And so, the cycle continues.

4. The Excuse Maker

This one comes up with reasons why you shouldn't do something. Or why you should delay doing something. All the reasons why you are not to blame, by deflecting blame or getting defensive. This is rooted in fear and keeps you "safe." But it also keeps you complacent, in a status quo mentality. For example, if you try to get promoted and don't, the disappointment would be too much to bear. The excuse maker steps in and tells you all the reasons you should stay exactly where you are.

5. The Perfectionist

This version is cunning. It tells you that you are never good enough. You never reach perfection, so disappointment always looms around the corner. Because we typically produce good results, we think striving for perfection is positive. But there is a high price to pay for being a perfectionist. Motivation through fear has ramifications such as stress, disappointment, and energy drain, to name a few.

Maybe you can relate to this story: Laura prided herself on the standards of practice she'd developed over years of work. She drove herself to produce the highest level of work in everything she did, setting a very high bar for herself, both at work and home where she ran the household. Her efforts were so tireless that she naturally drew attention to herself.

She was offered a high-paying position she thought would validate her. Unfortunately, it didn't work out that way. She didn't accomplish what she claimed she would. She began to feel like a victim of her circumstances and believed she was alone without help. She spiraled down into helplessness and eventually was asked to leave the job. This experience shattered the perfectionist image she'd worked years to create.

After much reflection, Laura began to realize she had options she'd overlooked; her need to control her situation had clouded her ability to see that. Her perfectionism worked for her until her work was so out of balance it stopped working. Her need to do everything perfectly ended up causing her to miss more important areas, like people.

How many strive for perfection when good will suffice. And the energy involved in that constant need to be perfect has a cost. At some point, you will pay it.

These damaging mindsets might offer a sense of protection from harm or an illusion of confidence. Perhaps they do provide this in the short term. But not for long. If we are unconscious of these thought patterns, they can lull us into a false reality where we become stagnant and eventually stuck.

Only you can create the life you want, consciously and intentionally. Even though outside events—from the unexpected loss of a loved one to the damage caused by a hurricane—can seem to rob you of full control over your life, only you can determine what happens next. Instead of letting a calamity derail your dreams, use the experience to drive you forward with even more courage and determination.

Giving power to negative experiences fosters more negativity. If you refrain from labeling an experience as good or bad and simply learn from it, you won't empower.

Instead, you'll walk away stronger by simply learning from it.

COPING MECHANISM PERSONAS—REACTORS

The mindsets above describe types of limited, negative thinking. How does this thinking impact how we react and behave in the world? How we cope, make sense of our situations, our behaviors. When we encounter stress or an obstacle, we resort to coping mechanisms we often learn in childhood to handle relational or interpersonal and environmental situations. They taught us how to navigate and survive each event. Although our coping mechanisms may have been helpful when we were kids, some of them may not be as effective or useful to us as adults. They may even work against us.

I've encountered seven typical coping mechanism types in business, although there are many more.

1. The Victim

The victim coping mechanism keeps the world outside by positioning a person as helpless to others or to circumstances. It keeps us stuck where we are and limits how we view the world. The call of the victim sounds like this: *I can't do anything because of these things that are outside my control;* or *I'm trapped without options in this job that I hate.*

2. The Blamer

The blamer goes a step farther and assigns fault to other people, places, and things and lacks ownership. One researcher states blame is the way we discharge our discomfort with our current internal environment. This may intrude in a variety of ways, for example: (1) *If I had a better boss, I could do my job more effectively,* (2) *If my co-workers were more organized, I could complete my project on time,* or (3) *My team is disorganized, so I have to do their jobs and mine; of course I can't get it done in time.*

3. The Disengaged

This coping mechanism keeps life at bay. We detach from our emotions because we don't care—or don't *want* to care—about the outcome. We might not feel like we can impact the outcome. Our voice isn't heard anyway, so why bother speaking up and staying engaged? We've checked out!

4. The Passive-Aggressor

Someone who is passive aggressive wants to be liked and thus will be the "yes" person, the one who needs other people's approval, the people pleaser. But an internal battle ensues, and they resent the position in which they find themselves. They might backhand a person, place, or thing. You'll notice this when a co-worker says, *yes, yes I'll do it,* and then doesn't and doesn't follow up. There's just silence. (It's easier to recognize this in another person than in ourselves.)

5. The Procrastinator

The **procrastinator** resorts to inaction as a way of controlling the situation. It's safer not to engage in the activity than to engage with potential unknown results. Uncertainty isn't a friend. These are people who commonly miss timelines or are scrambling last minute to complete a project, resulting in less-than-top-quality work. You can't count on them.

6. The Negative Naysayer

The **negative naysayer** prevents change by discounting any potential, new idea. Typically, this coping mechanism uses negativity to thwart change efforts because change is scary and uncertain. Fear drives the negativity.

7. The Lecturer

This person tells everyone what to do or what they should do. Pride leads, knowing everything and confidently sharing that with everyone; however, seldom does the lecturer listen to anyone else's opinion.

These coping mechanisms are useful when it comes to keeping change in check, for maintaining the status quo.

Take a look at this list to identify your most frequently used coping mechanisms. Do any of these prevent you from operating courageously and with excitement when facing change? If it's difficult to identify your coping mechanisms, enlist a trusted friend or coach to help.

Our coping mechanisms, like our thoughts and feelings, drive us closer to our goals or move us farther away. Eliminating less-than-helpful coping mechanisms leads to courageous, more joyful experiences in life. In essence, you're acknowledging and taking control of fear.

REFLECTIONS

Takeaway: Your thinking, emotions, and actions create your life.

Choose your attitude, thoughts, and behavior.

We all have coping mechanisms.

Self-awareness leads to conscious choices.

List some of your own takeaways.

JOURNAL

- Where is the resistance that stops me from assuming full choice of my life?
- Where do I feel I'm a victim to my circumstances?
- Who in my life provokes me to feel I have no choice?
- If I were to take one idea from this chapter and incorporate that into my life, which one would that be and why?

CHAPTER 3
DEFINE YOUR FUTURE

"The best way to predict the future is to create it."

—ABRAHAM LINCOLN

Defining what you want is the first, most important step, yet it's the one least likely to happen. Defining all aspects of our lives is hard—and people avoid it—because the very act of living gets in the way.

Life tends to move ahead at warp speed (especially if you have children), and most of us spend much of our day on autopilot, moving from one task to the next. You may be juggling work with preparing meals, interacting with your kids, and chauffeuring them to all their activities. Whatever stage of life you inhabit, your tasks may be different, but you still have daily demands. Now is the time to ask yourself what you really want (besides peace and quiet).

Define the life you want to create for yourself. If you don't clarify what you want your life to be, you may not be thrilled with the results. As I go through this process with my clients, it is typical to focus first on defining what they do not want, which may be a natural place for us to turn. But as I guide my clients in the direction of what they do want, the dialogue changes and they are much more energized with the outcomes.

CONTRAST CREATES CLARITY

How much time do you invest in exactly what you want versus what you don't want? When you catch yourself saying, "I don't like my manager" or "I don't want . . ." you fall into the mind trap. This is the opposite of what we need to do, and yet our environment trains us to dwell on the negative.

In and of itself, the negative isn't bad because the contrast provides a clear picture of what we don't want. So once we determine what we don't want—the contrast—we need to consider what we do want. To create the life we want, we must consider our thoughts, feelings, and actions because those determine our life.

YOUR WHY

Mark Twain said, "The two most important days in your life are the day you are born and the day you find out why."

Living our why fulfills us.

Given that premise, what do you see in your future? As you explore in detail what it is you want, focus your attention on that because we create what claims our focus. The why is critical to this process.

Have you spent time considering what your purpose is—why you're here and what you have to offer that's unique to you? What legacy do you want to leave? Often there's a strong correlation between why you want something and your purpose. What inspires your passion?

Is there anything at work that really excites you? For some, it's the relationships we form at work that keep us engaged and eager to succeed. For others, a good leader has gained our loyalty. Still others know having a strong cause is one way to increase engagement at work.

If you haven't ever thought about your purpose, or if you haven't been able to figure it out, consider what wakes you up in the morning and makes you eager to jump into the day. When we feel engaged and passionate about what we're doing, we're fulfilled. Certainly, there will be bumps in the road, but overall, we feel good about the work we're doing, the positive impact we are having.

I met a dear friend of mine years ago at work. At that time, she was a superstar in the role she had. Although we no longer work together, we remain close. She's now a mother of three, one of which has special needs. Her job is head of household, and her desire to be the best mother and wife she can be is what drives her. She's one of the most passionate, fulfilled people I know, and she has a very clear idea about her purpose. Her energy for life is endless.

What energizes you? Is it a specific job? A project or a company? Or is it to be a great parent? Whatever your dream may be, start by creating a list of what you want the most, then begin adding details to your list. If you're searching for the perfect job, write down some details that would make it perfect.

As I mentioned before, when you start jotting down what you want in a job, you may find it's easier to jot down what you don't want. Even though you're focusing on the dream job and its attributes, your mind may wander to what you don't want. Use the contrast to help you identify and specify what you do want. When you journal, though, write about those attributes attractive to you, the ones you desire.

For example, do you want a job that requires you to travel, or would you prefer to stay in an office with co-workers surrounding you all day? Do you prefer working remotely? Do you want to own a business, or do you prefer to have a consistent salary as an employee? Do you want to work for a large organization or a start-up? Are you energized considering working for a non-profit or a for-profit company? Be as specific as possible.

Now, tie your emotions to it. If you were to land that job with all the specifics you listed, how would it make you feel and why? Be extremely detailed here. The why is really important.

Why do you want to lead a family within which you have mutual respect and a hefty balance of fun? Why do you want the job that will allow you to travel the world? Why would that be fulfilling? What would it do for you if you had that job?

Journaling is a great way to foster more ideas about what it is you want. Free writing can be cathartic as well. It doesn't have to be much. Perhaps only a few sentences will add additional context and detail around what you're trying to achieve.

If you want something, write it down. Feel as if you have it now. Follow through with the right thoughts, feelings, and actions, and it will come. It may not arrive tomorrow morning on your doorstep, but if you have faith and regularly put effort into your goals, you'll achieve them. Continue to gather your thoughts and experience the feelings you'll have when the outcomes you wish to produce are already here. (This is where daydreaming is okay.)

Years ago, in my struggle to find my perfect job, I journaled. I described details and created a dream (vision) board to reflect that. Part of my criteria was this job would find me in less than sixty days. I had no idea what kind of jobs were out there in an industry with which I was unfamiliar, but I knew what I wanted to do and described it with specificity. During this time, I looked for opportunities and continuously acted in ways to support my vision.

Visualization and journaling are important. Equally important, though, was the research I did to find jobs containing those components on my dream list. Visualization, journaling, and action go hand in hand.

In less than sixty days I landed the perfect job. It was everything I'd written down in my journal—which I didn't even realize until I picked up the journal almost a year later. As I read my description of the "perfect job," I realized I was in it. I found it! Not only did this reinforce my approach, but it increased my confidence that I could actually accomplish this. Let me tell you, this works!

Visualize, journal, and search for opportunities to take action. The journaling provides you with a reference, a historical snapshot. As you master this fluid process, refer back to what you wrote previously to learn what changes you require. You can use this vision boarding process for a dream job, a new relationship, or any other goal you hope to achieve.

The root of the why begins to address the source of your fulfillment, which is the indicator we're doing what we love—or not. There's no magic in this process, but if you are true to your inner compass, you'll find fulfillment.

Consider the dictionary definition of fulfillment: the achievement of something desired, promised, or predicted. If you want to be fulfilled, the first step is to clearly define what that means for you so that you can create a fulfilling future.

Once the clarity of the what and the why are in place, the next step is how. How do I get there? Keep your eyes open for opportunities to ask for help (one might call this research). For example, when I decided I wanted to write a book, I had to consider who to ask for help. I had to figure out the first step. These inquiries and/or online research provide fuel for you to continue on the path toward achieving it.

It's normal to experience fear during a process like this, so don't let it stop you or hold you back. When you decide you want to do something new, crazy, or outside the area you think you could achieve, fear shows up through your thoughts or inner critic. Go into this knowing this, but keep moving forward anyway. Surround yourself with ideas and people who support your dream and remember this process starts with your thoughts. Think about what you want, then attach the why to it because the why arouses your emotions, which leads to the how and the what. Look for opportunities to take action.

REFLECTION

Takeaway: We create our own life with our thoughts, feelings, and actions. Clarify in detail what you want and why it's important and include some thoughts around how you will proceed. Elucidate what fuels your passion. Look for opportunities to take action.

List some of your own takeaways.

JOURNAL

- What is my purpose? My why?

- What are my short-term and long-term goals?
- What is my perfect job, or what is my idea of a perfect relationship?
- Why do I want those things? (In other words, if I had this, would I jump out of bed each day, eager to start?) What thinking do I need that will bring me closer to my dream? If you could create your future, what would you do? What elements would you include in this perfect situation? Be crystal clear when you describe what you want, and don't jump ahead until this is complete.

CHAPTER 4
DEFINE YOUR STRENGTHS

"We delight in the beauty of the butterfly, but rarely admit the changes it has gone through to achieve that beauty."

—MAYA ANGELOU

Three colleagues at their company meeting discussed how they were consistently left out of projects compared to their peers. They suspected this was due to the exclusive and biased behavior of decision-makers at the firm. Cheryl, who had been with the firm the longest, felt defeated and that perhaps she didn't have the skills and experience the team needed. Her colleagues and friends pushed back on that notion and suggested this new norm wasn't due to their lack of skills or strength.

Still, the flagrant bias hurt each of them. In fact, it made them angry. Because they hadn't experienced this level of exclusion with previous employers, it took a toll on their confidence and self-worth. However, as they discussed their options, they didn't want to resort to anger or the feeling of defeat. Instead of being victims of circumstance, they wanted to imagine how to improve themselves and their work environment. Together, they exchanged feedback. They shared what they believed were the strengths of each person present so that each would have that outside perspective. What had begun as a negative exchange turned into a valuable discussion. Each one left the conversation more confident in their worth and the value they brought to the job.

Some of your experiences may have left you feeling undervalued, but it's important to remember we're each born with unique gifts. As we grow, we experience areas in which we flourish and talents that expand. We find opportunities to do more of what satisfies us, and when we do, we're in our element. If you're reading this and thinking you may not have any unique talents, think again; perhaps this resonates with you, but you don't have time to focus on those unique qualities. Or perhaps you have a quiet voice within you that says pursue them!

Use this section to identify your strengths. What are your specific talents that have been celebrated in the past? In what ways have you personalized those talents to make them uniquely yours? (Perhaps you have a good sense of humor. Do you use that to diffuse difficult situations?)

If you're not fully aware of and anchored in your own strengths, then you may look to others and see theirs. When that happens, you fall into the trap of wishing you were that person or you had that person's strengths, qualifications, experience, wisdom, body, and . . . on and on. It's easy to lose focus on what you have to offer and instead look outside yourself to what others have to offer.

On the one hand, we can admire others' strengths to see how we can incorporate them into our own way of doing things. On the other hand, we can fall into a trap and tell ourselves, "Clearly I'm not good enough because I don't have that characteristic." And what a seductive trap it can be.

When you fall into that mire, your negative thinking takes a mud bath. Your inner critic finds all the reasons why another person is more qualified, educated, and just all around better to the point that you come to believe that clearly you're not good enough. Imposter syndrome is real and takes a toll on our confidence. Self-doubt is pervasive. When you fall into this trap, you can totally lose focus on your own worth and your strengths. Don't get caught in the quagmire of desperation and despair, and guard against adding a dose of perfectionism, which will complete the mud bath as well as thwart your ability to clearly see the path that lies ahead. Discipline is required to keep your focus on where you shine.

Maybe you have a difficult time discerning what makes you a unique, important member of society. One way to begin the process of identifying these traits in yourself is to ask for feedback from your peers, relatives, or subordinates. Ask them what they perceive to be your talents and take what they say and create a list: your sense of humor, your ability to remain calm in a storm, your tremendous attention to detail, your organizational skills, and so forth.

Those specific strengths you (and others) have identified form a brand, so the next step is to identify your brand. Are you the one to whom people turn to for very creative solutions, or are you the one who knows how to foster relationships within a group?

ASSESS YOUR ASSETS

If you struggle with identifying your strengths, you may find value in a third-party test, such as 360s, StrengthsFinder, and StandOut, just to name a few. Not only will these tests reinforce what you may already know, they can also unveil new insights you hadn't previously considered.

After taking the StandOut assessment test, I found I'm in the line of work now that supports my strengths (after twenty years of trying to find where my passion lies). These results simply reinforced what I experience when I'm living my dream. There's likely a correlation between your strengths and your purpose, so when you find your purpose and live it, you feel fulfilled. Below are the links to the StandOut Assessment and to StrengthsFinder.

https://www.tmbc.com/standout-2-0-assessment/

https://www.gallup.com/cliftonstrengths/en/254033/strengthsfinder.aspx

As you continue to assess your assets, be honest about who you are, your skill set, and what you need to move forward. Never stop learning. One executive reported they have a philosophy of lifelong learning. Another mentioned he reads, studies, takes classes, and speaks with other leaders to stay current in his field. Like these successful people, continue to grow in ways that support the areas in which you want to excel, understanding we're never a finished product. Ideally, find an organization that supports employee development programs. Thankfully, so many companies understand the benefit of continuing to cultivate their people. I've spoken at many organizations where they have leadership certification programs. Their identified high performers are encouraged to complete classes, at the end of which they're certified. Many companies offer coaching to their leaders. Take advantage of those programs your organization has to offer. If you're currently seeking employment, ask during your interviews what development programs they have in place for employees, as well as if there is tuition reimbursement for graduate programs. There are many opportunities to build your skills because companies understand having these programs in place builds their employee bench strength, making the companies more competitive in the marketplace.

Once you've defined the life you want, the company where you want to work, and the role you want to take, you can start to identify areas you need to develop to be competitive, always keeping your eyes open for opportunities. It's easy to fall into the trap where you become mired: "Well, if I only had this skill, I could interview for that job," or "If I had this experience, I'd definitely put my name in the hat; but because I don't, I won't," or "I don't have time." Make the time—you're worth it! Research has illuminated men are much more likely to interview for a job for which they have less experience than women. That's a differentiator. As you've probably often heard, "Fake it till you make it." Neurologically, we need to build new neural pathways. So we practice new thoughts and actions until those pathways are built, and we become more comfortable operating that way. Many times, a great attitude and a zest for the challenge wins over experience to give you a seat at the table.

REFLECTION

Takeaway: My strengths are my brand.

Those with whom I work are a resource for feedback.

I can take a strengths-based test for third-party validation.

Needing to be perfect holds me back from living life (and may also hinder the lives of others).

List any other takeaway for yourself.

JOURNALING

- What do I love to do?

- What are my strengths?
- How will I identify them? From whom will I ask for feedback?
- Can I be honest with myself and embrace my strengths?
- In what areas do I refrain from participating because I think I may be "not good enough?"
- What skills do I need or want to develop or enhance, what books do I need or want to read, or what courses do I need to take to help me attain the position I want?

ALIGN

CHAPTER 5
WAKE UP YOUR LIFE!

"Every choice starts with a decision. Every decision starts with a thought. Every thought starts with a preconceived idea. It is up to you to decide what you do with each, but always remember that the choice you make will result in the consequence you face."

—KEMI SOGUNLE

CONSCIOUS BALANCE

Before I propose my approach to balance, let me preface it with this: In business, the norm was that you were supposed to show up as your professional self. In relationships, you're supposed to leave your business at the office. In physical and mental health, you're supposed to deal with these ailments by going to the doctor and taking a pill (or two or three). We segment off pieces of who we are and expect to be just a portion of a person. *Stuff those other parts of you until you get home (or you are home; and you finish work).*

I've seen people who suffer from illness come to work and hide what they're experiencing. I went to work with cancer while going through a divorce simultaneously. I hid my pain. I thought if "they" knew, they'd exclude me from work, so I hid—as others have before me and likely will after. Maybe you can relate. In the last several years, states of overwhelm, anxiety, and depression are more common/prevalent due to the fact we spend so much energy hiding who we are and what we are going through.

And so, balance. Everything we do, everything we are, and everything we have experienced make us unique with our own wisdom and perspective. Balance is out of whack when we focus on pretending to be something or someone we're not. Balance is out of whack when we show up to work pretending we don't have feelings or that we have to be "nice" to everyone because it's expected but not deserved. Balance is turned upside down when we stay in an unhealthy relationship. We do this because we have a warped belief that to stay in an unhealthy, unfixable marriage prevents our children from being hurt. We pretend, we hide, we manage, but inside, many of us are crying and feel so completely alone. There's no balance on that path.

What if it became common practice—not just common sense—to "be me," to be who we are all the time without apology? What if we accepted every part of what makes us unique and ugly and beautiful? What if we released the shame, guilt, embarrassment, and perfectionist standards to accept and love who we are, as we would a child?

We'd free up all that energy to redirect toward problem-solving and innovation. All the energy we waste on fearing exposure, coping, and defending ourselves, into creating the life we've always wanted, living our "why." All the energy we use fighting and defending our value, toward greatness. Imagine waking up and living a fully conscious, balanced life.

At eighty-two years of age, my mom has balance. She eats well, she has a healthy weight, and she takes no medication because she has no ailments. She exercises, meditates, and prays every morning. She's dealt with the experiences in life that have caused her pain, and she's forgiven those who hurt her. She holds no resentment, nor does she hide who she is. Drama comes into her life via other people, but she can allow it to pass like the wind. My hope is I don't have to wait until I'm eighty-two to have consistent conscious balance.

WARRIORS

We are complex, superhuman beings who multitask, nurture, strategize, create, love, solve, mentor, provide, protect, and so much more . . . on a good day. On a bad day, we can throw some (or all) of those qualities into the closet, say "to hell with it," and fight and compete like cutthroats. The key is to embrace all parts, not just the acceptable ones.

Think of it this way: One day, when you leave the house, you know that at some point you'll meet Henry Cavil or Charlize Theron. Do you decide to leave the house in your flannel pajamas, mouthguard on, no makeup, your hair a mess, and say, "Honey, come here!" Likely not. We much rather dress to the T, smell incredible, and have the wind blowing in our hair, a soundtrack playing in the background as we walk down Sunset Boulevard.

That's symbolically how many of us go to work or relate in our partnerships. We want to present ourselves as all put together. However, we may not have dealt with all our emotional issues from childhood or the dysfunction in our family or the current shame we feel. Sadly, though it remains unacknowledged, everything leaks out into the world around us. Furthermore, we load our bodies with fast food and give up exercise, only to wonder why our bodies are revolting against us with disease. And when we meet with conflicts because we haven't taken care of ourselves holistically, we overreact. Feeling ashamed of our behavior repeats the cycle.

Physically and chemically our bodies work with us or against us. Being out of balance leads to negative ramifications for our body and mind. We're more reactive, less patient, and have less control over our behavior. The state of imbalance doesn't help our brand at work or with our relationships.

Our daily life is filled with conscious and unconscious choices. When we thoughtlessly compartmentalize our life (into any of these parts—work, relationships, and health/wellness), we ignore parts of who we are. It's as though we're asleep at the wheel. If we ignore any portion of ourselves, we're less in control of how we think and act and are more likely to inadvertently say or do something we regret.

For example, you've been multitasking all day and still need food for dinner. You rush through the grocery store and yell at someone who cuts in line instead of letting the person step in front.

At work you have so many projects due you struggle to keep your head above water. As you sit in your workspace (which may be home) completing one of the tasks, you're distracted by interruption after interruption. You're torn between picking up your kids, taking care of animals or elderly parents, and completing your day job. When your direct report calls to ask for help, you explode, and he makes excuses to hang up quickly. (Oh . . . and now you remember you forgot to eat all day.)

We are warriors attempting to complete everything in our lives at 100 percent. Of course, in the process we sometimes suffer from the demands we put on ourselves. For us to find moments of conscious balance, it's important to attend to three major areas in our lives.

First comes taking care of our bodies, our **health**. This includes what we eat and drink, as well as the spiritual practice to nurture our soul. Exercise keeps our stress levels down and our hearts healthy. Our bodies are our sacred home. They take care of us when we take care of them.

Next is nurturing our **strengths** and embracing areas where we need attention.

Finally, nurturing our **relationships**—with ourselves as well as those we love. Consider how to be more present with those who require energy and focus.

Life moves extremely fast (except when we feel badly and it seems to slow way down). If our tendency is to complete the list of tasks, we can miss making conscious choices. I call this sleepwalking through life, sometimes just to get by. But as warriors, when we *wake up our life* and create the life we've always wanted, watch out! This world will be a better place when each of us wakes up to make conscious choices in all areas of our lives, putting our best self forward instead of sitting in the corner.

HEALTHY MIND AND BODY

What we feed our bodies determines how effectively they run. It's not reasonable to strive for perfection when it comes to eating, but it makes sense to be mindful and consciously choose the food we eat. Know your body and what foods make it operate optimally, and which foods do not. I can't eat a candy bar or donut in the morning without feeling physically awful. I get a quick sugar high and a headache, but then I want to fall asleep.

Our food choices impact us emotionally as well as physically, both of which are important as we look for balance. We can choose to eat at Burger King frequently and then complain of being overweight. (Of course, our weight isn't at fault, or is it?) If we eat fast food and then feel shame or guilt about our choice, was it worth it? Would you feel better emotionally if you chose something healthier? After years of weight and emotional swings caused by unhealthy eating, I decided to choose my food wisely. This doesn't mean restricting my food, but rather being selective and aware (see the reframe). If I choose to eat pie, I don't feel guilty afterward. I just don't do that to myself anymore. The guilt and shame we put on ourselves directly related to body image damages our state of being, our energy.

This is why mindful eating is so important. Unconscious eating impacts our overall health and balance. When you make conscious choices about your food, those unwanted, self-deprecating emotions are less likely to arise. When we experience shame, guilt, sadness, or anger, it oozes out onto family members or workmates-—or both. We're more reactive when we don't support our bodies by eating well, exercising, and using some form of meditation or journaling for self-discovery.

Stress adds fuel to the reactive equation as well and increases cortisol levels, which over time is detrimental to your immune system and overall health. So physiologically, when we're stressed, our emotions are heightened. It's easier to fly off the handle.

Fast food, lack of sleep and exercise, combined with chronic stress are an invitation for disease to find its home in your body. Some people are sensitive and feel the effects of stress on their bodies immediately; while for others, it may take a while for high blood pressure or high cholesterol to present in our bodies. The pharmaceutical industry thrives because many of us go through life taking pills to solve our problems. It's estimated in 2020 we spent 1.27 trillion US dollars on pharmaceutical revenue worldwide.

Here's the rub: When we're so busy, it's tempting (and easy) to make poor choices—to eat what's easily available, skip exercise, and allow no time for introspection and meditation. Prepare, think ahead, and support yourself so that you're making good choices for your future. Notice which foods energize you and which make you feel poorly (whether physically or emotionally). When you're low on energy, remember how exercise makes your body feel. Do everything you can to make it easier to choose the right thing for your health.

Finding balance when it comes to your health is so important, and yet there's no cookie-cutter approach to achieving it because balance depends on you. There are factors that you can include or exclude from your life to support your everyday quest for balance, but it's personal. Some factors proven to influence the brain's ability to cope with stress are whether you eat properly, exercise daily, and provide your body with adequate sleep—all of which are so much easier said than done.

Many gurus recommend meditation for a healthier mind because it aids our ability to improve self-awareness. The following are tips and tools to create the best outcome for your personal meditation.

Meditation apps like Calm or The Tapping Solutions allow for a ten- to fifteen-minute (or as long as you desire) mindfulness break. These breaks help you stay centered when things go off-kilter.

Be silent for five minutes every morning and when you go to bed. Clear your mind. Then set your mind as you would a clock. Appreciate what's good in your life, that for which you're grateful. This is called intentional discipline.

Focus on those aspects you want to increase. If you want to be rich, appreciate all the bills you've been able to pay this month rather than focusing on the deficit. Thank yourself for all the work you do to earn your paycheck so that you can pay those bills. That may seem silly, but you're focusing your mind into gratefulness. This is the way to achieve what you value and what you want to increase.

A calm mind supports being balanced. When we have this frame of mind, we're less likely to be impatient and critical. An attitude of gratitude improves our flexibility: we're less likely to be intolerant of people and situations when we have a happy, grateful frame of mind. When we lose that peace of mind, we open ourselves to impatience, intolerance, anger, disappointment, and feeling overwhelmed. Trust me, this isn't fertile ground for balance!

PROFESSIONAL BALANCE

Take a minute to think about how you show up at work. Are you leading and influencing others as your best self? In working with organizations for many years, I've witnessed strong leaders and dysfunctional ones. Strong leaders seek to improve themselves and are humble enough to embrace those areas in which they need to improve. There's a level of transparency and integrity that sets them apart from others. They embody courage.

However, consider this: We all grow up in families with some level of dysfunction. Maybe we're yellers, or when we communicate, we don't tell the truth, manipulating others to get our point across. Maybe one parent is the dictator and everyone else cowers. So many family dynamics are at play when we're young.

Now, imagine repeating that behavior over and over again until it's fully ingrained in us by the time we reach adulthood. Unless we're very aware or have had therapy to work through our family dynamics, they'll dictate our interpersonal patterns. That means our organizations are filled with hundreds of different family dysfunctions that haven't yet been processed and replaced with more effective behaviors.

As adults, we bring to work both effective and not-so-effective relational behaviors. Fear is one behavior I see frequently. The fear of the unknown leads to a resistance to change. Fear can also be found in a resistance to open, honest communication. It may be a fear of hurting people's feelings, retaliation, or being excluded.

When speaking with groups within organizations, I frequently hear, "We have a nice culture." There's a value to being nice to others, but the cost is truth. The definition I've created regarding "nice" behavior is: "I'll be nice to you, but in return, I expect you to give me what I want. If you don't, I'll be passive aggressive and show you that's not how the game's played." Nice behavior can be motivated by the need to please people. People pleasers sacrifice their truth to make people happy. There is a huge cost to this.

When we use our energy in the pursuit of pretending and hiding what we really think, we don't have energy for other, more effective ways of thinking and acting. If unchecked and unconscious, these dynamics cause us to overreact, to say things we regret. Balance is showing up fearlessly in support of self and others in a respectful way. Balance is being the authentic person you are, your best self.

RELATIONSHIPS

In superhero form, we try to accomplish everything. Most work from home or a hybrid model, run the household, and are results driven. Maybe you're in the ideal position where you love what you do, you fulfill your "why," and love your role. Whatever position you're in as a friend, mother, father, or lover, you're likely juggling priorities.

That feeling of overwhelm can set in quickly if you're not keenly aware of its approach. Understanding how you cope with being overwhelmed demands self-reflection. For example, perhaps to release anxiety, you clean or shop.

For years, I was in an unhealthy marriage from which I had to disengage emotionally to survive. When I realized what I was doing, I knew my marriage would have to end. I didn't understand the impact that disengaging had on my relationship until later, but I know when life got hard, that was my coping skill. What's yours? Having this awareness allows you the space to accept and embrace who you are, and to hold healthy boundaries so you can have moments of balance.

CHOICE

Ultimately, the way we treat our bodies, the foods we eat, the way we interact at work and in relationships, the stress we allow to negatively affect us, and our emotional state influences our chance of disease, but we have a choice. Sometimes it doesn't feel like we do, but we choose how to respond to people and situations in our life. We choose the food we eat. We choose how to care for our bodies and our minds. We choose to overreact or take a breath and pause.

The question is whether we prioritize self-love and compassion. Are those two nurturing attributes at the bottom of our list, or do we make them a part of our daily routine? Our decisions result in our effective or ineffective ability to cope with work and our relationships, ultimately impacting those around us. So when we feel stuck, like a victim, and give in to that feeling, it affects not only our state of being and energy but that of those closest to us. We're all connected to one another on this planet, and how we treat ourselves and others matters.

You do have a choice to *wake up* and create a conscious life.

REFLECTION

Takeaway: You're a whole person everywhere you go.

Stop hiding who you are; instead, use that energy to create your desired life.

Wake up your life and make conscious choices to empower the working, relatable, healthy person.

We create a healthy, balanced lifestyle—or not—based on our choices.

Use tools such as the Calm app or The Tapping Solutions app to support quick, mindful moments throughout the day.

Balanced nutritional choices and physical activity produce optimum health.

Unprocessed experiences from childhood can leak out when we least expect it.

Mindfulness is a choice. Incorporate some type of quiet time to process the day. Self-awareness is needed globally.

JOURNAL

- Are there any places or relationships in your life where you hide who you are?
- What tools can you utilize throughout the day to support balance in your life?
- Have you made choices recently that have betrayed your peace of mind?
- What could you do differently in those situations to create a better outcome?
- On a scale from 1-10, where are you now relative to balance (10 being complete balance, 1 being completely out of balance)? What would make you a 5? What would make you a 10?

CHAPTER 6
ALIGN YOUR MINDSET

"Nothing is impossible. The word itself says I'M POSSIBLE."

—AUDREY HEPBURN

There's no denying that challenges, obstacles, and change are part of life. For instance, years ago I was speaking to a woman with whom I worked and respected, and we were discussing the elements of work we didn't appreciate (including people). As we talked, we uncovered why some of the experiences bothered us, and the whole conversation seemed rather bleak.

As we concluded our call, though, we openly discussed the negative discussion and how it left us feeling "judgy" and bad. I offered that sometimes it's important to process through what's bothered us and why we didn't feel good after those experiences. We uncovered what we didn't like and value, which directed us into a discussion of what we really did like and desired for the future.

We took the conversation in a positive direction, discussing what we wanted in the future that would make us feel awesome! We both left the conversation clear about what our own next steps were as we moved to creating what we wanted in our careers.

Take a moment to consider a time you had a job you loathed (maybe that's now). It uncovered the aspects you don't want in a job, didn't it? Unfortunately, that's where so many put their focus—on the unwanted elements. Instead, try reframing what you've learned into a positive statement of what you do want.

When you're reading a novel, you expect the main character to encounter obstacles that get in the way of the desired goal. In a book, that goal is fairly clear. In life, however, it can be rather murky. Although we anticipate obstacles to arise in a story, we're often surprised when they occur in real life. We fall victim to these circumstances quickly. Giving into thoughts such as, "There's nothing I can do about that. I guess I have to give up," can make the goal twice as unlikely to achieve. Important questions we need to ask ourselves, "In this situation, what can I control and what outcome do I want?"

If you embrace the contrast surrounding us and accept that the less *and* more desirable outcomes are always possible, you approach tough situations with more flexibility. We have to understand what's good and bad in each situation in order to appreciate what we want or wish to avoid.

You cannot create your life and be a victim of it. The empowered mindset is the premise you create your future with your thoughts, attitude, emotions, and behavior. We all encounter situations where we find ourselves asking, "Why did that happen?" Maybe it's only in retrospect you see how your actions (or inaction) caused a poor outcome; or your attitude got in the way.

You've probably heard the saying, "Find something for which you can be grateful." There's merit to that. When you look for areas in your life for which you're grateful, you're shaping your attitude. The more evidence you see of good around us, the more you continue to find. It's a looping process, and it reinforces what you want and actively shapes a positive, grateful frame of mind. When we have a positive attitude, we make better choices. We no longer see ourselves as a victim but as a designer of our own life instead.

To make this clearer, think about people who are so negative you avoid them. Have you ever been to a meeting where individuals are complaining and blaming? It creates a negative feeling, doesn't it? (Have you been that person?) Being in proximity of negative people can weigh you down, and their negativity is infectious. When the mind is rampant with negativity, we lose the ability to see clearly. In fact, if you have a negative disposition at the moment, you may be looking for someone to reinforce that. But how does that end? You feel good temporarily, but you don't get any closer to the positive outcome you want.

Like attracts like. The only way you can begin to attract positives in your life is to switch the dial on your attitude to positive. As I tell my kids, have an attitude of gratitude, a mindset that is so important I reiterate it throughout the book. If you focus on negative events, people, and experiences to justify your position, that's where you stay. Even if positive events occur in your life, if you have a negative mindset, you'll miss them.

This is what a victim statement sounds like: "They always blame me for being so negative and derailing the meetings. I am just telling the truth."

Here's what it sounds like when you're not a victim: "Boy, I feel really misunderstood. What am I saying or doing that's causing this outcome? What am I missing?"

See the difference? The first statement is from a victim perspective; the second statement is from an empowered perspective. You choose which perspective you want to operate from. You always have a choice.

Recognizing that we choose our attitude is the next step to creating change. Find opportunities to bolster and shape a grateful, positive attitude.

Once we acknowledge our response or reaction in any given situation, we begin to actively choose how we want to show up. This choice is what determines the life we create. There's a difference between controlling life and creating the life you want. I see many individuals and leaders try to control their people and their surroundings. The problem with this is the motivation for their actions. The motive of control is fear. The misconception is that if you control your life, then you leave less to chance and uncertainty. Life is uncertain though, and change is constant. As a leader and an individual, we need an element of trust—trust that your people will deliver, your life will turn out well, and that change is for the better.

I'm not saying sit back and watch. You must be an active creator in your life, but again the difference is motivation. Are you coming from a place of fear? Are you trying to control others? Or are you coming from a place of trust and love? Are you actively defining and pursuing the life you want? Do you support the people who work for and with you?

RECOGNIZE AND CHANGE THE DIALOGUE

Do you recognize when your thoughts are turning to doubts?

How do you know if your thoughts are supporting or hindering you from achieving your goals? Likely, because you're human, you have times when they support you and times when they don't, but what's the split?

Learn to recognize self-doubt by wearing a rubber band on your wrist. When the voice of self-doubt speaks up, snap the rubber band. Just as we give a child a time out to reconsider their choices, give yourself a time out when the story turns ugly.

Once you recognize the negative thoughts, you have a choice: Do you stay negative or change the story and become (at least) optimistic? If you allowed yourself to be a director in your internal dialogue, what would you like the script to say?

Next, keep track of how often your negative thoughts prevailed by placing a tick mark (indicating negative thinking) on a white board or sticky pad. If you find you've only slipped once or twice, good going! If you have several check marks, however, consider the events that occurred that provoked your negative thinking and be aware of where your mind is.

Keep track of your negative thoughts in this manner every day for a week. Can you recall what triggered your negative thinking? What did the negative talk in your head tell you? Did it hold you back? Did it prevent you from action? If so, it might be because of a survival mechanism built into us, a voice suggesting we should be afraid and not go into battle. It's our fight-or-flight response.

Humor is another powerful tool to defuse negative emotions and help you change the narrative.

Early on in my career, I worked with a group of people I would call friends. Our meetings with the president always ended with him yelling at one of us. It was so stressful because we never knew who had the bullseye on their head during that meeting. We would try to make light of those meetings by suggesting we sing during the meeting to derail the yelling. We would all end up laughing at the thought of it. It would deflate the anxiety we all felt walking into the meeting.

Another method you can utilize when the situation turns dire is **stop, drop,** and **roll**. When a negative story is playing out in your head, **STOP**. Recognize it's a negative narrative and stop it. Next, **DROP** this story and reframe it until it's at least neutral, but better yet positive. Finally, **ROLL** with your new positive version.

For example, your boss gives a directive to you and the team. The narrative in your head turns into something like this: *The directive must be a result of my failure. The last time we had to do this project, the approach was different. He must have modified it to dummy-proof it because of me.*

Using this method, STOP to recognize you're creating a potentially damaging story based on your fear of inadequacy. Consider you don't know why the directive was given. Reframe it in your mind and decide his instruction will benefit the outcome of the project and may even be a result of some comments you made. DROP the old, damaging narrative and replace it with the new one without assumptions. ROLL with the new story. When you're creating the new narrative, it's not wrong to double-check with the person to see if there are any beliefs working against you of which you should be aware.

Reframing your thoughts enables them to line up with what you want to achieve, but this requires discipline and awareness. Imagine in detail what you want to create as a perfect future. If your thoughts and actions aren't aligned with that vision, it won't happen.

Another method is to take an outside position and listen to what it's telling you. For example, it may tell you, *you won't do well in that job interview. You're not good enough.* Or maybe it will say, *you're not good enough to compete.* Listen as if you were dealing with a child because we're likely to be much more compassionate with a child than we are with ourselves. Ask the thought, *what are you trying to tell me? Is it a message to protect me? Is it a message to hold me back from the unknown because that space is too scary? What would my situation need to look like for me to feel safe?* Once you've answered these questions, give yourself permission to let it go.

Changing your mindset and emotions also elevates your energy. Here are some ideas to do this, or come up with your own list so you have a tool when you are in a low energy, negative state.

Some of my activities include watching an uplifting YouTube video, like America's Got Talent episodes with the underdog doing something amazing that no one expected. Or a Dr. Joe Dispenza real people testimonial. I love taking Bradley Rose, @bradley_rose23, on Pelton. He makes me laugh the whole ride. My go-to activity is to read something uplifting or call a friend. Just don't catch yourself in the trap of telling the same story, which reinforces the negative feelings and pain. I do yoga (thank you @RossRayburn), listen to a meditation, and watch a Star Wars movie (just to name a few).

These activities break the looping negative narrative and lift you back up to a place of possibility. From that elevated state, you can decide what you want to think and how you want to feel.

REFLECTION

Takeaway: Recognize if your thoughts are in line with your goals.

You can't reach your destination with your foot on the brake.

Align your thoughts with what you want to achieve.

Utilize tools to recognize and stop the negative chatter: Stop, Drop, and Roll.

Notice the voice of the inner critic and take an outside position.

JOURNALING

- How often is my negative chatter present?
- How frequently do I notice my inner critic conveying negative, hurtful messages? What triggers the inner critic?
- Any themes in the messages?
- Was I able to change my mindset from negative to something lighter and more positive?
- When does the gremlin typically rear its head?

CHAPTER 7
ALIGN OUTSIDE IN

"Our deepest fear is not that we are inadequate. Our deepest fear is that we are powerful beyond measure. It is our light, not our darkness, that most frightens us. We ask ourselves, 'Who am I to be brilliant, gorgeous, talented, fabulous?' Actually, who are you not to be? You are a child of God. Your playing small does not serve the world."

—MARIANNE WILLIAMSON

I was proposing a new business idea during a meeting. When I left the room, two people remained. They closed the door after me. My mind started racing with self-doubt and the potential conversations they were having about me.

How often does your mind start racing with all the possibilities, which are usually negative? You can spin yourself into a space not helpful to you or your goals. Perhaps, you move into one of the Reactor Personas.

I waited for my emotions to stop swirling before I headed back into the office where one of the colleagues was sitting behind his desk. "I noticed you both closed the door when I left," I said simply, "and my sense is there was a 'meeting after the meeting.' I want to know if you have any feedback for me on the meeting we just held?"

We ended up having a good conversation, and I left with a concrete direction for my next steps. Had I not asked the question, I could still be pondering the many different dramatic scenarios I'd concocted in my head.

This is the essence of *outside in.* Taking outside events as material to create assumptions inside your head.

What people or events in your environment can influence your current thinking and outlook? Are your thoughts directing you toward your goals? How can you use those thoughts as indicators to inform you of the direction you're headed?

It is much more typical for people to insert a negative narrative in the gap of missing information. To assume is human. To negatively assume is common practice.

One executive I spoke to described an experience he had with a colleague who he later found out spoke poorly of him at every turn. That person who spoke poorly of him left the company, and six months later, the executive was promoted. He strongly believes the reason he was held at a standstill was this person's bad-mouthing, and when that person was gone, his path was clear for the promotion.

Are there people and experiences holding you back? Why are they and what can you do to change it to be in charge of you? What are your intentions? Are they positive, or are you being manipulative—or worse, deceitful? This chapter is about learning how to recognize what's happening inside you by looking at the people and experiences around you as indicators—*outside in.*

UNCOVERING OBSTACLES

One way to uncover the way people see you is to consider the situations at work. Do you feel included or excluded? Years ago, when I worked for a company and had just had my second child, I felt excluded from the cliques composed of young, single people (or partnered people without families) who would grab drinks after work. I, on the other hand, would race out to pick up kids, grocery shop, cook, and clean until the next day when I'd sit in meetings and feel as though I'd missed conversations . . . because I had—at the bar the night before. Knowing what I know now, I could have conversed with one of them to find out what they'd discussed, what I missed. That would have made me look interested, and I would have learned more about what was discussed that was pertinent to my job.

What might be holding you back and stalling your forward momentum? Use your environment to discover the lens through which people view you and use that as feedback.

I worked with a team of leaders who stated one of their gaps was effective communication with another division. They relied on this division to execute and deliver their service. This team was very clear that they were good communicators and the other people were the problem. "If they could just get their act together, then things would be good," they told me.

When faced with the question, "What can you do to improve the situation?" they said they'd tried everything, and this other group really was at fault. This leadership team I spoke to felt stuck, as though they were victims of this situation—so much so that some in the group tried to hold back tears. They couldn't see they had a choice in this situation.

How often have you felt stuck in a situation or with a person, like a manager (or maybe a husband or wife)? You felt as though you'd tried everything, yet the problem continued to exist. You decided, "They must be at fault!" That decision can move quickly into a downward spiral.

Confirmation bias is defined by the *Oxford Language Dictionary* as *the tendency to interpret new evidence as confirmation of one's existing beliefs or theories.*

We look for experiences to confirm our belief that we're stuck, and of course, we find them. Even if they're not real examples, we twist and change the story so that it fits our narrative.

When information is missing in a story, it's easy to fill the missing parts with a narrative, which is typically negative and certain to confirm our own bias. For example, your partner was supposed to be home at seven o'clock for dinner, and now it's eight thirty and they're still not home. This may have happened several times and you feel disrespected, not important. You begin to imagine your partner's not paying attention to the time and that they're having fun at work or with someone else with no regard for your dinner plans. You may wind yourself up into a tizzy and become very upset: you can vividly picture your partner doing this to you; you haven't heard from your partner, you have no idea where they are, but you've created a full story to explain why they are late. Then your partner comes home, and you let them have it. The situation escalates into a fight where no one's happy. You find out later the story you concocted in your head was inaccurate: they had a flat tire, forgot their cell phone, and were miserable, just wanting to come home to you. Unfortunately, upon their arrival, you created a firestorm.

Although creating this narrative is our way of protecting ourselves, it may bring about bad situations. Furthermore, it's unfair to those we attack. If we're unaware of what we're doing, we'll continue to craft stories to fill in missing information and keep ourselves in a victim state. Since we choose the narrative we create, opt instead for a neutral story to fill the gap of missing information.

I've heard it said that when we feel like a victim or we feel stuck, our brains start to limit our problem-solving ability. So physiologically, we spiral down and become more "stuck" unless we have a tactic to help us when we find ourselves in these situations.

TOOL TIPS

A tool to use when emotions are high and a negative reaction to a situation is imminent is to "Take Ten." That means digest what happened for at least ten minutes, if not more. Try to remove the emotion from it and try to see the other person's perspective and why they made the decisions they did. When you're ready to address the situation, be sure you can do so without heavy emotion attached. If you need more than a ten-minute time-out, and if seeing the other person's perspective is tough, then follow the steps below.

1. View the situation. Recall it with as much accuracy as possible: What just happened? (Imagine you had to accurately document all sides involved.) How did you react?
2. Assess the meaning. What is the real significance now? Is there a need to follow up? If so, what outcome am I trying to achieve? (Do I want to rip the person apart or have them learn from the experience?) Pay close attention to your motivation as that directs the results you achieve.
3. Become curious. Why did the people react the way they did? Start asking good questions—not leading, judgmental ones. This takes you out of the seat of accusation and puts you in a place of being open to hearing what really took place.

4. Bring it to conclusion. What will you do now to create the best outcome, acting with grace and respect? Even if you disagree with the other party, you can be respectful. If you were to achieve the desired result, what actions would you need to take to get there?

If you follow these steps, you'll achieve greater success when those less-than-desirable moments happen. If all else fails, obtain an honest perspective from a person you trust.

LOVE OVER FEAR

Life, of course, *happens* at work and at home. How we react in each situation determines whether the outcome is favorable. While battles in business are common, challenges arise, and I strongly believe we must support one another. Tearing each other down at every opportunity to move ourselves ahead of others is counterproductive. The old folk adage seems to be true: what goes around comes around. What you send out is what you'll receive in return.

Throughout my career, I worked with great people, and I worked with people who haven't found their inner moral compass. Years ago I worked with a colleague whom I thought was on the same page as me and connected with a similar vision. While attending a small business meeting, her words betrayed her, and her true agenda became apparent. I was dumbfounded since we had been talking about our shared vision. I thought we were aligned. In the meeting, however, she steered the conversation in a direction that was not in support of our previous conversations. It was a mouth-dropping moment.

If each of us enacted a personal code of honesty, respect and kindness (different from *nice,* which I referred to earlier) in every organization, we would flourish. We'd have one another to lean on when things got tough. We'd be able to ask the tough questions and trust we were going to hear the truth. We'd be able to grow to the next level of development because there would be a foundation of trust. We could hear the hard things about ourselves and work through them.

This effort requires tremendous courage and a willingness to be vulnerable. This type of code to be genuine with one another so that you can each develop and grow to your fullest potential is leading with love.

We live in a spectrum of energy, thoughts, emotions, and behaviors. On one end of the spectrum is love while on the other is fear. The love energy can include emotions such as gratitude, recognition, appreciation, caring, and thoughts which are focused on acceptance, forgiveness, appreciation, compassion, and love. It can also include self-nurturing and self-care as well as care for others. (I am not referring to self-centered or narcissistic love, which is rooted in fear. Rather this begins with self-love, kindness, acceptance, and respect.)

On the other end is fear. Those emotions could include feeling a lack of, less than, not good enough, anger, jealousy, revenge, and hate. Thoughts could include I am not good enough, I am bad, they are bad, judgments, and/or they are trying to hurt me (or I want to hurt them), which makes them bad. Neutral is in the middle of the spectrum. We may not even notice this as it does not necessarily capture our attention.

When we give compliments, appreciation, or recognition to someone, even if only in our thinking and heart, we are coming from the love end of the spectrum. We are giving and in-service to others. When we withhold love or focus our intentions and thoughts on perceiving others in a negative light, we operate from fear. Each end of the spectrum creates a ripple effect, and with it, consequences.

A good leader has tremendous skill and experience. A great leader has that *plus* the ability to consider people along with business results. And finally, they listen to their intuition and humbly lead with all these qualities.

Leading with love may be a foreign concept to you. But the notion of leaving your feelings at home is antiquated. One big shift from the pandemic: people no longer tolerate poor leaders, those that lead from fear.

Leading with love is strong, not mushy. It's grace. Leading with a foundation in love, through self-awareness and curiosity, is strength. If you are curious regardless of the challenges that arise and the ensuing emotions that follow, you know how to harness and lead through these difficult, trying times and inspire others to follow. You can rally your team and help them align with the end result. A leader with an intention of love has the right balance of transparency, accountability, and vulnerability to communicate effectively emotions that may be present during challenges and unseen obstacles. This allows space for others to be authentic, have their voice heard, and reduce potential reactivity under stress and pressure.

Leaders mentor people; they coach their employees and build them up.

The opposite of love is fear.

Discrimination is a byproduct of the real problem, which is fear. Fear is limiting, judging, tearing someone else down to lift yourself up. It's dishonesty to get a win, having power over someone else, comparing, being critical, stealing someone's work and calling it your own. Fear is gaslighting and having narcissistic traits. And finally, it's not having the courage to be honest because you fear what could happen. It is passive aggressive. This can manifest as someone trying to be "nice" because they are too afraid to be honest; they'd rather say what their listener wants to hear and then go do what they really wanted to do behind their listener's back. Fear is having a strong belief that you identify with, and therefore, you exclude others who do not hold that same belief as you or think like you. You are closed to others different from yourself because you take it as a threat. You are not authentic because your self-focus narrative tells you it will limit your career, so you act or play the game.

And fear doesn't have to be negative. Fear holds you back from asking for a promotion or a pay raise. Or fear stops you from getting a health check because you sense the news will be bad.

When fear is present and you succumb to it, then likely you have a repeating story in your head driving your actions. That negative or fear-based story steals your energy and your peace.

You can also have fear, recognize it, lean into it, and do the right thing anyway. That is empowering.

REFLECTION

Takeaway: We tend to fill in gaps of missing information with our own story, which is typically negative. Fill the gaps with facts before fiction.

Your environment—people, situations—are indicators of obstacles that may be perceived or real. *Outside in*. Use these indicators to define your potential next steps.

Be the driver of your journey, not the backseat passenger.

JOURNAL

- What is my environment telling me about how people see me?

- Are people holding perceptions about me that may be working against me?
- What actions can I take to move closer to creating alignment with my goals?
- If there are situations at work in strife, go back to the first step.
- **Define**: What outcome do I hope to achieve in that situation?
- Then **Align**: What do I need to think or do to create that outcome?

DESIGN

CHAPTER 8
COURAGE

"Rejection is merely a redirection; a course correction to your destiny."

—BRYANT H. MCGILL

The Design step is the final step in creating your desired outcomes. To work this process, reflecting on what you've accomplished thus far is helpful and insightful, so I encourage you to document your progress. The Design step requires you to focus on what you need to do to continue your journey, no matter where you are. You may find you need to modify your goal due to unforeseen circumstances, so be flexible as you approach completion.

Have the chutzpah to keep going, even if you can't see the finish line—that's courage. Act as though you've already achieved the outcome you desire—that's confidence. Then keep going—that's consistency.

COURAGE

Recently I watched Reese Witherspoon interview Dolly Parton in her Netflix series *Shine On with Reese*. When describing her success and what it took to get there, Dolly recalled a story of her early years in Nashville. She came from a large, poor family and moved to Nashville when she was eighteen to establish her talent as a songwriter and a solo artist, founding her own publishing company to maintain the rights to her music.

One of the early songs she wrote was "I Will Always Love You." Elvis Presley was coming to town to record his music and wanted to include her song. She thought, "How amazing! I'm going to meet Elvis, and he's going to sing my song!" The day before he was to sing it, his people informed her he had to have the publishing rights to her song. She said "no" to Elvis and was heartbroken when she learned he wouldn't sing her song without owning it. She cried that night, but she stuck to her guns and kept her copyright.

Years later, Whitney Houston sang that song, which became a huge hit, and Dolly felt proud of how the song sounded through Whitney's interpretation. Dolly's courage to stand her ground was what made that possible. Where do you need courage in your life to support your goals?

Over the years as a coach and a speaker, I've spoken to many leaders and have asked to what do they attribute their success? Their answers included good coaches, mentors, trusted friends, and great teams, but what struck me was an overwhelming theme of being authentic and humble. It takes courage to be authentic to who you are. They said they were willing to be wrong to get it right. They continued to ask and were open to learning. They did the right thing, even if their knees were shaking. This is courage—to be wrong to ensure you achieve the best outcome.

Do you have strong people in your life to whom you can turn, who will be honest with you? Will they tell you when they think you have it wrong? Do you have the courage to listen?

Courage is a prerequisite to achieving your desired life, just as it was with Dolly Parton. Courage propelled her toward her dream of being a successful songwriter and solo artist. To have courage, one must deal with fear—fear of change and the unknown. Fear is often an obstacle to our forward movement. Whatever the reason for the fear, if desire causes us to forge forward, then we need courage to propel us. Self-doubt takes a toll and can easily derail you from staying the course.

Rather than seeing rejection as negative, capable of robbing you of your dream, accept it as a course correction, what Bryan McGill refers to as "redirection." That's a powerful interpretation because it assumes courage. With this mindset, you find some interesting turns along the way that you didn't anticipate.

Think of an airplane flying from Los Angeles to New York. It doesn't fly a straight path; it takes a curved route, flying where the traffic and weather are the least likely to interfere. When our course takes an unexpected turn, we need to roll with it and refuse to be discouraged. When a course takes that unanticipated turn and we're questioning the direction, many people give up; but it's exactly at this point that you need courage to progress toward your goal. Use it as a learning moment.

Courage and faith are the traits required at this stage. Courage enables you to imagine and dream and really *feel* it's going to happen. You must believe, even when your negative talk can try to hold you back.

In movies, we love the hero who demonstrates unbelievable courage against all odds. We especially appreciate the hero who continues the quest, even though they could potentially lose everything they value. The greater the risk, the more we love the hero for doing what's right. Why? Because we know how painstakingly hard it is to do what's right when many would take the easy path. There's always the character that tells the hero, "No one would fault you for walking away," yet we root for them to continue their pursuit, living vicariously while hoping beyond all hope that they triumph.

This is the faith required to walk into the unknown, onto the uncertain path. You'll hear the nagging doubts, yet you must continue anyway. Faith is required to continue with hope and a good attitude where you believe you'll achieve what you set out to do. Believe you'll achieve!

I use my social media accounts to keep me focused on my goals. Because many people with whom I'm connected provide motivational quotes or stories, those help me stay focused on my dream. When others share their stories or quotes that talk of perseverance regardless of the obstacle, it gives us hope. Never forget to tell your stories so others can derive hope from you.

I also have a "Happy" folder in my email box that contains messages from past clients who have thanked me, quotes that touch me, and stories to motivate me. I look at this folder when I need support.

I am surrounded with people who are working to achieve their dreams, so we support each other. It's easy to get sucked into those relationships at work that are gossipy and focused on drama or negative stories, but those won't help you move forward. Stay focused on what you want to achieve. Water what you want to grow. If you want more drama and negativity in your life, then continue to hang out at the water cooler and gossip. But if you're interested in making a change, achieving what you've not yet achieved, then find new people with whom to surround yourself.

It takes self-reflection and courage to be transparent. Relating to people without hidden agendas is a critical part of building trust in a relationship. Associate with people you can trust and who are trustworthy. Search for the win-

win in your relationships. You may experience fear when being transparent because it requires a level of vulnerability; but friends who are trustworthy provide the space for you to be vulnerable without judgment.

DISAPPOINTMENTS AND FAILURES

Winston Churchill said, "Success is the ability to go from one failure to another with no loss of enthusiasm." Doing this requires courage.

Garth Brooks has a song that's impacted my life many times called "Unanswered Prayers." There is a line in the song that says, "Some of God's greatest gifts are unanswered prayers." Think back on your life. Perhaps you had a crush in high school, and you so desperately thought you wanted to date that person—maybe you even prayed you could date them—but it never happened. Then you go back to your twentieth high school reunion and you see that person holds absolutely no interest for you now and vice versa. At this point, you'd think, *Thank God for the unanswered prayer*. We can't always catch a glimpse of why something didn't go our way, but a level of trust and willingness is required to learn in these circumstances.

If you interviewed for a job you didn't get, trust it wasn't the right one for you and then do your due diligence. Ask questions of the interviewer: "What could I have done better or differently in the interview? What was the deciding factor that ultimately led to your choice?" People rarely ask such questions, but they're so valuable to our development. Through questioning, we learn and improve so that when the right opening occurs, we'll nail it.

We may not always get our desired outcomes when we want them or in the way we want them, but when you ask for feedback, each circumstance is an opportunity to grow and improve. When you do ask, simply listen, take notes, and then say, "Thank you." Take that information and inspect it; share it with a friend and ask their opinion. The information and feedback are gold, and it's how you continue to understand where your strengths are and how people perceive you, then you can cultivate your brand. When disappointment happens—and it will—document it. What did you learn, where are your opportunities to improve, and where did you shine?

Lastly, when you encounter perceived failure, you can choose how to react in the situation. Your choice is to assume the worst or assume the best. Many times, we're faced with situations where we're not given all the information. For example, if you weren't given the job or promotion, you might be tempted to fill that gap of missing information with a narrative, which is typically negative. You might say, "I don't know why I didn't get the job. Another candidate must have been better than I." We assume the worst, and sometimes we become so good at it that we may even create a story around it: "I really bombed the interview. They must have found a candidate who was really clever and nailed the interview. They probably had lunch together and connected, laughed it up. And I struggled. I could never be as good as that candidate."

Alternatively, we could choose a positive narrative to fill in the missing blanks: "I didn't get the job. I'm going to ask for feedback in an email to find out what I could have done better. Next time, I'll be prepared with a story that demonstrates how I overcame obstacles to show my perseverance. This experience makes me better for when the perfect job does come along. I'll nail that interview and land the job I really want." Look at disappointments as life's course correction.

This is when you need both courage and discipline. It's not always easy to stay positive when your course is corrected, but you can set yourself up for success by having an activity to support a positive mindset when events don't go as planned. For example, I'll call my friend who already knows what to say when I lose courage because I've prepped her ahead of time. She knows what I need to hear. Or I go on a long walk and clear my head, listening to music. Or I cook a new recipe I've been wanting to try. What would help you keep a positive mindset? This approach allows you to continue the journey.

You're defined by how you handle yourself in the face of disappointment. It's easy to be positive when times are good, but the moment life goes awry, that's when the rubber meets the road. The way you think and react to a person or situation is key. Do you handle your perceived failures with grace? You can be disappointed inside, but your words and actions demonstrate grace.

An excellent example of grace in challenging, unfair times is illustrated in the movie *Hidden Figures*. All three women meet obstacles that none had faced before—much less overcome—yet they handled themselves with grace and dignity in adversity. They always behaved respectfully with their supervisors because it was the right thing to do. They handled themselves with grace and dignity during the most frustrating times and stayed the course, ultimately pioneering the way for others. Imagine if they'd given up or yelled at their boss, calling them "good for nothing" just to stick up for themselves. It was because of their grace, dignity, and perseverance that they reached their goals—and ultimately improved technology. When faced with challenging people and circumstances, it's easy to want to respond with a fight. But with the focus on "what outcome do I want," is that the best approach?

You can ask how the project could be improved and learn from it. You can be disappointed, but your words and actions demonstrate grace. We live in a time where we can be honest with grace, stick up for ourselves, and ask for feedback when we don't understand and are receiving any level of criticism. Furthermore, building one another up supports us being even better. If you're receiving anything less, ask for feedback.

REFLECTION

Takeaways: We need courage when the unknown is in front of us.

Transparency is a healthy form of authenticity.

We need self-reflection to lead from a place of strength.

There are always deviations to our plan. Course corrections are a part of life.

We have a choice as to how we approach change. Our attitude will define future choices.

JOURNAL

- Where do I need courage most in my life now?
- What would it look like if I moved forward with courage in this situation?
- Is there an area in my life that requires my attention that I've been ignoring? Where?
- Do I handle perceived failures with grace?
- Have I recently experienced a directional change that requires a shift in the way I view it?

CHAPTER 9
CONFIDENCE & CONSISTENCY

"The four Cs of making dreams come true: Curiosity, Courage, Consistency, Confidence."

—WALT DISNEY

Confidence is important when applying for a job, following your integrity, doing what's right, but even more important, to be a strong leader. People follow confident leaders. It is the main ingredient in having *executive presence*. They're not so likely to follow someone who openly demonstrates self-doubt. If you feel as though you're lacking confidence, focus first on the negative self-talk and identify what messages are taking you off your center. Reframe those messages and move forward like the leader you are (or want to be). Some of us may not see that in ourselves, but it's time to find your value and move forward. Imposter Syndrome (lack of confidence) is widespread. Some of the most brilliant people suffer from Imposter Syndrome.

Competence is an accumulation of skill, knowledge, and experience in a certain area. Confidence requires a belief in oneself, having self-trust and self-esteem. There are some differences in gender related to confidence, although the lack of it can strike any of us. Research supports the idea that women need to feel fully competent in a skill before they'll feel confident. However, many men don't require a high level of competence to feel confident. (If this resonates with you, read *The Confidence Code* by Katty Kay and Claire Shipman.)

Furthermore, when open positions arise that require a certain skill set, men with low competence in this area but high confidence often pursue the position. On the other hand, women with high competence may see themselves as needing to further develop their skills and thus have low confidence, which means they won't pursue the position. Thus, more men acquire executive positions and leadership roles in the framework of competence and confidence, which leads to men taking roles they weren't equipped to lead.

Maybe you are not a woman, but lack of confidence and how it impacts you resonates. At what point can you accept your competence and move forward? Do you need to have a 60 percent competence level . . . 90 percent? So the question remains: What will it take for you to embody self-confidence? When is enough, enough?

One step we can take is this: if you see someone struggling with a lack of confidence, HELP! We're stronger together, and when we help each other, especially in this area, we're also helping ourselves. It's a win-win. The person needing confidence gets a boost from your support, and you feel good for helping someone in need.

A friend of mine is an entrepreneur and just starting to work in a new area of business. As we were discussing her approach, she was struggling in one area: money. She felt very uncomfortable with her new pricing model. It was so much more than when she worked in nonprofit, but it was in line with what her competition was charging. The only difference between them and her was she hadn't built the confidence around this increased pricing model.

As we continued to discuss it, she cringed, thinking about how she'd tell this potential client about the cost. Yet many colleagues told her it was standard practice. She knew she needed confidence in this area and creating the confidence to have these conversations was integral to her ability to move forward. It didn't matter how many times I told her she was worth it; she needed to change her belief system.

After many pep talks, role-playing, and strategizing how she would approach money with this client, she had the conversation. She defined the outcome of the conversation she desired, then she aligned her words to create that outcome. She called me after her phone call with the client and was absolutely ecstatic. She said the conversation went really well, and the client didn't push back on the price at all. She needed the confidence to have the conversation, and in this case, she reframed her thinking, focused on the outcome, and delivered the message accordingly.

OWN IT

One way to embody confidence is to own your current and past choices. It's easy to own happiness, joy, and a feeling of fulfillment, but what about when we're angry, resentful, and hurt? When we own our hurt as our choice, we embody confidence. What would people do if one day we all decided to own and embrace all aspects of our being our authentic selves and joyfully paraded around as who we are and not the façade of who we want the world to see? The world might not know what to do with us, but we'd be happy!

Learning from our mistakes helps guide us in the future. Years ago, I was miserable in a role I'd been hired to fill. I felt leadership was jerking me around, I didn't have support, and my boss was two-faced. I was ultimately asked to leave that role, which relieved me and made me happy.

When I think back to that position, I should never have accepted the role. Instead of dealing with that decision head-on, I let it linger and left it up to chance. I now own my lack of leadership and direction in that position and the misery I felt. Ultimately, I believe my misery came from the fact I didn't feel equipped or supported to complete it. I felt like a victim. I should have owned that then so that I could have moved into a more empowered position of leadership, which I needed to succeed.

I learned a hard, valuable lesson. In retrospect, instead of holding a grudge against my boss, I should have owned my choices that resulted in an unwanted consequence. Because of this realization and because I now own the experience, I've changed my course in life and am now empowered to build up others. I'm controlling my destiny instead of ceding control to circumstances or another person. We create our future one choice at a time! Sometimes we even have to generate our confidence in order to move forward.

You may encounter people who seem to be determined to prevent you from achieving your goals. When it becomes obvious to you, it's easy to fall prey to self-doubt and into the role of the victim. Your first response may be fear and anger, so simply acknowledge these feelings so that you can move beyond them. Doing so enables you to decide on your next move from a place of clear thinking and a centered choice.

Focus on the outcome you desire and work backward. Decide what steps are required of you to get that desired outcome.

What doesn't kill us makes us stronger, and I feel like there are a lot of strong people out there!

CONSISTENCY

All three steps—Define, Align, Design—require consistency. Even though your course may take some unexpected turns, don't give up. Instead, remember to follow these tips:

Redirect: Your course may change, but keep your focus on the desired outcomes. There will always be deviations or, at the very least, surprises. Glue yourself to the goal.

Reframe: When you encounter something that appears to be an obstacle or a disappointment, you simply need to reframe it. Consider this example that happened to me.

Years ago, I proposed an idea I wanted to have come to fruition at work. The team wasn't on board with my idea, and I could tell they wanted to move in a different direction. My initial reaction was disappointment, and I spent a few minutes discouraged because I was really passionate about this idea and wanted to see it birthed. I was concerned about one person who I thought was trying to sabotage it.

At that point, I recognized what I was doing to myself: I was creating a scenario of this person's intentional interference in my plan and starting to wind myself up. Fortunately, I caught myself and reframed my thinking about the situation. I dug myself out of disappointment and positioned myself into a place of curiosity. Perhaps there's a better place for my idea to manifest itself—if not here, then somewhere else. I'm looking forward to seeing this happen and will look for opportunities to build it elsewhere. This is an example of reframing.

Resist: A temptation to quit may rear its ugly head. You may feel stuck when you can no longer see how you'll achieve your desired outcome. RESIST! Don't give up hope. Surround yourself with others who are optimistic. You can always find reasons or excuses for not reaching your goals. Instead, surround yourself with those people who energize you and your dreams, those who are also seeking ways to fulfill their goals and dreams.

Remembering these steps helps us maintain a consistent attitude as well. Keeping positive is so helpful to having a mind that's open to new possibilities and new directions.

The second part of consistency is about you, your words, and your actions. Think about how you evaluate people and their performance. Typically, we judge people based on their words and actions, yet we judge ourselves based on our intentions. It's important that you focus on what you intend to do and then execute. If you say "I don't like gossip" and then spend all your break time at the water cooler gossiping, people neither know your intentions nor hear your words but instead see your actions. They'll judge you based on your actions and not on what you intended to do.

Just as athletes are judged on their consistency, so are we as professionals. If an athlete has an amazing game once in a while, they're not as valuable a player as one who is consistently able to perform. In the same way, if you meet your deadlines 40 percent of the time at work, it's likely that those around you won't have confidence in your word. If you want to be viewed as a valuable performer who honors your word, be consistent. Do what you say you'll do.

Being consistent seems so simple, yet when I'm working within organizations, I hear this as a common complaint. People have excuses for why they couldn't meet their original deadline. The bottom line is that we'll be judged on what we say we'll do whether or not we do it. To be a credible asset within your organization, honor your word and be consistent.

People find comfort in knowing their colleagues will do what they say. Our friends feel the same, and this is how we build trust with one another. Thus, when something occurs unexpectedly, our knee-jerk reaction may be to get angry. Instead, it would be wise to remember the three steps: Redirect, Reframe, Resist.

MEASURE SUCCESS

One way of measuring success is to note the milestones we've completed or the major obstacles we've overcome. If an obstacle is more like a pebble on the path, you may not recognize the win, but even the small wins should be recognized and celebrated. How often do we simply continue to look to the next milestone in our journey and neglect to stop and celebrate the win?

What's your measurement of fulfillment? Someone once said, "If you can't measure it, it doesn't exist." One way to track your progress is to reread your journals, look at your vision boards, and remind yourself of the affirmations you created. This is another reason why journaling is so important. Not only is it therapeutic and sets in stone what you want, but it also captures a specific moment on which we can reflect and determine where we've made progress. It's important to look back to the words written and the boards created because that's when you know you achieved what you set out to create.

When working with a new coaching client, I provide them with a series of questions to respond to and journal about. By the end of our coaching time together, we reflect back on what was most important for them when we started and where they are currently on the journey. There's much to be learned when we document our thoughts, hopes, and dreams, when we have an opportunity to process and work on those and finally reflect on our progress. Responding to questions such as, "What would I do differently having gone through that?" and "What did I do really well that I want to repeat?" helps us take the time to measure our progress and recognize our efforts, which provides comfort, confidence, and fulfillment.

Fulfillment is a sense of achievement. No matter how small or large the task, when you accomplish it, you should feel fulfilled. As I work with groups, there's a tendency to focus on what needs to be accomplished and to overlook what was completed. I've yet to meet individuals and teams who feel they receive way too much recognition. Let's make this a priority. Achievement of progress needs acknowledgement, which leads to the sense of fulfillment.

I think there's a false sense of how fulfillment feels. I can assure you it doesn't involve trumpets sounding, balloons falling, and us living in the happy-ever-after. We may feel euphoric, but that's not a permanent state of being. I think fulfillment is achieved when we recognize what we've accomplished, moment by moment.

Look for evidence of the people, experiences, and events in your life that are supporting your dream. You may see something grab your attention on the internet or a friend may reach out with an opening that's the job of your dreams. Realize dreams can continue to morph as you continue to desire new adventures. The sense of fulfillment is within you, and it simply requires you to tap into it daily.

REFLECTION

Takeaway: The most important part of this equation of measurement is to celebrate the wins, no matter how small. Because life moves at a rapid pace, it's so easy to skip over those moments in which you realize you completed something important to you. Review your day to keep track in your journal, reread your journal to look for evidence of your accomplishments, and then celebrate. Recognize yourself and honor your efforts. Make the time to share your accomplishments with a friend who will support your efforts. Finally, recognize those people in your life who can use appreciation. Let's build each other up. We can do so much more when we do it together! What doesn't kill us makes us stronger.

Confidence is generated within; no one can give it to us.

Confidence and competence are intertwined.

If you see a person needing confidence, help them.

Your path will change directions, but consistently keep your eye on the outcome. Be a source of consistency so that people can depend on you.

Add value by honoring your word.

Rejection is simply a course correction.

One way to perceive success is to look at the obstacles you've overcome.

Recognize progress and celebrate the wins.

JOURNAL

- What experience has made me stronger?
- What does it take to make me feel more confident?

- Where in my life do I need confidence? What steps can I take to "fake it till I make it?"
- Is there a situation that's recently occurred that I need to redirect, reframe, and/or resist?
- Where are my consistencies? List my consistent attributes.
- What is one thing for which I'm grateful that occurred this past week?
- Today?
- How would I define fulfillment? Now imagine I'd accomplished everything on that list. Can I experience that fulfillment as I imagine it?

CHAPTER 10

LEAD FROM YOUR AUTHENTIC SELF

"To be yourself in a world that is constantly trying to make you something else is the greatest accomplishment."

—RALPH WALDO EMERSON

Many leaders I speak to have a strong desire to be authentic. Whether they are in a meeting with stakeholders, running an offsite, or interviewing for a new role, they are committed to being authentic.

Remaining authentic to ourselves in business requires us to follow our inner moral compass, which may neither be easy nor popular. If there seems to be a right and a wrong, choose right. This is powerful. Some of the toughest decisions we face require us to choose a path at the fork in the road.

I have had many leaders complain of their struggles to be authentic while navigating the politics that could lead to them being liked—and even more important, getting a promotion. Many see this struggle as an either/or.

Being authentic in a world constantly trying to make you something different requires long-term vision and grit. One path may lead to short-term power that requires bringing others down in order to elevate our own status or position. Another path could be to stay silent while witnessing an employee backstab another co-worker. Or worse yet, staying silent while you are being gaslit by your boss. All of these scenarios have a cost and an imagined pay-off. Allowing your boss to shame, manipulate, and gaslight you is the cost (and the pain and damage that is connected to that); the pay-off you tell yourself is that if you tolerate it, maybe they will give you a promotion, for example.

While the right path might feel shaky and will require massive amounts of courage to choose, you know in your gut it's the right choice. When you choose this, it reinforces the decisiveness, bravery, and power you have within you. You know when you've listened to your gut and when it's been ignored. Here are some examples clients have shared with me:

I was interviewing people for a position that would report to me. I found candidates that could "do the job," but I found one who was amazing. I was afraid that amazing person would make me look bad and even, worst-case scenario, take my job, so I ended up hiring one of the people that could just "do" the job.

I was in a meeting with our president who asked about a project and why it was not complete. I told him that it was the marketing manager's fault for not getting it done. I pointed the finger. I could have chosen to share some of the roadblocks which confronted us, and how it was nothing short of amazing that the project was still as far along as it was. Instead, I made my colleague look bad so I would look good to the president. Technically, I didn't do anything wrong . . . but my gut felt like I was sucker-punched.

I was interviewing for a new position within my company, and I knew others were vying for it too. I was asked questions that put me in a position of having to choose to elevate myself by pulling others down and I fell for it. I put my colleagues down so I would look good but felt awful when I left the interview.

I shared vital information with my colleague that was critical to the success and new direction the organization wanted to take. Unbeknownst to me, my colleague took that information as his own to the acting CEO, resulting in a promotion [for my colleague] and my termination. I left willingly without exposing my colleague, who I thought was my friend.

We all face difficult choices like the examples I shared here. Do we want to lead an authentic life and choose the right path, the path of integrity and respect? Are we motivated and seduced by our fears to choose the path requiring us to be less than decent, less than honorable? Movies always depict the main character having to make a tough decision: lead an authentic, honest life or lead a life that's deceptive, greedy, and power hungry. We root for the character who chooses the honest choice.

LISTEN TO YOUR GUT

Choices aren't always fun, easy, or clear, and making a choice often requires us to tune in to our gut. When I say "gut," I mean there's a higher power—one not attached to ego—inside each of us that's our guidance system. If we tune in, we can find the answers we seek. If we ignore it, we're left feeling less than. When we make poor choices, we may start to justify why we had to do what we did, which can spiral down into negative self-talk, lack of confidence, and self-doubt.

Anger is a response that's an easy lever to pull when we want to control our environment, but if anger's the first floor, fear is the basement. Fear is a motivator for anger and negativity, and all together, fear, anger, and negativity repel and take us farther away from our moral compass. These emotional responses create barriers between us and others and are reactive not proactive. Leading authentically requires thought, introspection, and self-awareness.

Live and lead from your authentic self; anything less is a façade. The problem of living a façade is it takes energy to maintain it, and that depletes your value. Being true to yourself is empowering. When you're tuned in to your moral compass, it will be easier to make the right or fair decision.

Have you ever squelched a thought or comment because you didn't think it would be popular? Consider this: if we ignore or push down thoughts or feelings because we believe they won't be popular or appropriate, they'll fester and burst at some point. I call it a stack attack. All the little things we ignore, push down, justify, or squelch start to build until one little thing sets us off and we explode because we're not addressing something or not being true to ourselves. Now, this doesn't mean you should go shouting from the rooftops, exclaiming statements of your truth, but it does mean you should listen to your gut and honor it with grace.

To lead an authentic life, you must own every aspect of you. Are you hiding your voice to preserve an image you want to project?

Being authentic requires bravery. My dear friend gave me a bracelet I wear all the time that says "be brave." It's my reminder in every situation that I must be brave, which usually requires me to take the tougher path. When you make the choice to be authentic, you become a stronger leader, stronger person. The more authentic you are, the more you condition yourself to decipher which decision is the right one in any given situation. For some, you may feel it in your gut. Others may sense it, or some may even hear it. Whatever it is for you, become good at listening to your inner wisdom in whatever form it takes. Listening to your inner voice of wisdom is a skill.

Mindful Moment

Close your eyes and think back to a time when you had a tough decision to make. Maybe it was a choice in your relationship or at work. What were some thoughts you considered as you weighed your options? When did you know that was the choice you were going to make? How did it feel in your body, and where did you feel it? What did the feeling tell you? In retrospect, do you feel you made the right and fair decision, or were you simply trying to be right?

REFLECTION

Takeaway: Our value has the greatest impact when we lead authentically. Measure today's actions by your authenticity ruler. Is this really who I am and who I want to be?

Anger stems from fear and pulls you away from your inner moral compass.

Bravery is living authentically.

List some of your own takeaways.

JOURNAL

- What does it mean for me to be authentic? Where did I shine? Where could I improve? What does my inner wisdom/moral compass tell me is important?

CHAPTER 11
ALL FOR ONE AND ONE FOR ALL

"We are only as strong as we are united, as weak as we are divided."

—J.K. ROWLING

I want to end this book with a message of hope, and with the possibility of what we can do to inspire hope for others and ultimately change the balance in the world.

My clients have been inspirations for me. Even when many of them have been in the face of terrible situations, they look to call forth their best self. This may sound logical, maybe even reasonable, but it is far from easy.

One such client was trying to get promoted. He was demonstrating all he anticipated would be important, galvanizing his supporters so he would be an obvious choice. And then it happened. His boss caught him completely off-guard in a staff meeting and lied to the team about his work, which was not his work, and he had to decide if he acquiesced, which would likely enable him to get the promotion or tell the truth and ruin his chances.

The predicament made him shocked and in disbelief he would have to make such a choice which could be career limiting.

A CEO I worked with found out her CFO had made a $5 million mistake. She was devastated and could not believe it. This was a tight-knit group, and she knew it would end his career there if not permanently and send a negative message about herself as a leader. How could she continue to lead when she missed such a huge, costly mistake? Her people would never truly believe in her again; on the other hand, if she kept it a secret, it would cost her the integrity she held as so important.

A leader who had big aspirations for his future had half his team quit due to how he led. He didn't understand how he had rubbed people the wrong way and wanted help to understand, but it would have been so much easier to leave this job and put it all behind him. He had a choice to make to give up and change jobs and hope this event would not follow him or to stay to ask for help and make the necessary changes. The second path was not easy because he couldn't understand what he was doing that had created such a negative impact on those that left, but he was committed to "getting it right."

In all of these situations, my clients made the choice to follow their inner moral compass, to lead with authenticity. The first client gracefully and courageously let the truth out in such a way that his boss did not lose face publicly, but he honored his integrity, and he did get the promotion. The second example, the CEO let her CFO go and also shared with the company the mistake that was made and started the repairing process with the people. She courageously followed her integrity to do what she felt was right. She eventually resigned.

The third example the leader was open, vulnerable, and changed his mindset and behaviors, always coming from love and integrity. He would tell you he had some dark days, but he came through a stronger leader and ultimately received a new role with potential for tremendous growth because he put in the work and stayed.

Making the right decisions is not easy. Many times, it's harder because you may not feel or see a payoff except for doing the right thing. But these are examples of showing up as your best self. Leading this way requires tremendous courage, patience, self-awareness, and integrity. The choices made by these individuals had ripple effects. They made choices based on selflessness, integrity, and being authentic. There is a ripple effect that occurs where others are impacted by the hard decisions, and in turn, they are inspired to do the right thing and so it goes.

Sadly, when we see the world through a lens of "in order for me to win, you have to lose" mindset and we focus on others, we tend to compare, judge, and become critical because of fear.

In this age, diversity and inclusion are at the forefront of change within courageous organizations that desire to improve their culture. While embracing difference is more prevalent than ever before, we still have miles to travel. When we judge others and ourselves, we limit possibilities. When we come from a place of fear, we limit the possibility of greatness. We can no longer afford to be critical or judgmental but must stand strong and band together to make a difference.

After day one of a diversity and inclusion conference in San Francisco (a city I love), I sat with approximately twenty other people at a dinner in a downstairs private room (which felt like a cozy cave). The host requested we introduce ourselves, state who we are, and who we work for, and "why" we're interested in spearheading the D&I effort. She also asked that we include "a brag."

As she kicked the introductions off, I was truly moved by her story as she set the tone for everyone else in the room to be equally vulnerable. She was at a crossroads in her business life and knew she wanted to be in service. She had a dream of quitting her job and going to Africa to help native girls in need. I was astonished by the tremendous vulnerability created amongst strangers, some of whom teared up when they stated their "why." While I was stunned, I was also so comforted.

We were all united by a cause: to better our company culture by creating an inclusive environment where all people are treated fairly and have a sense of belonging. We desire a culture where difference is celebrated and where people at all levels of a corporation value all people, not just some.

After dinner I walked—skipped—back to my hotel room and lay in bed wondering if we'd ever experience a time when this feeling of inclusivity would realize itself in business. My mind raced with all the possibilities that lay ahead, and I fell asleep with such a warm feeling, one of hope. The next morning, I was excited to experience day two at the conference and was blown away by the tremendous feelings of hope and possibility. We heard speaker after speaker describing their amazing work in the world.

One gentleman, Joe DeLoss, founder & CEO of Hot Chicken Takeover (he calls himself the head chicken fryer), told us he gives back to the world by hiring people with "alternative resumes"—people with a criminal record. Having a criminal record challenges any individual seeking employment, and of course, a job is necessary for rehabilitation into a community.

DeLoss shared he's developed a business staffed with loyal employees because he truly cares about giving back to people who may have lost their way and are now trying to reclaim their lives. He's pushed through the irrelevant traditional business model and created his own to support his employees.

For example, instead of offering a 401(k), he offers other benefits that are more important to his talent pool, such as salary advances for a down payment on a new place to live. His mindset is "How can I serve not only fried chicken but also people?" In an industry with a high employee-turnover rate (150 percent according to PeopleSoft reported by MIT Technology Review), Hot Chicken Takeover is incredibly low at 34 percent. This is only one example of what can happen when we're committed to being in service and creating an equal playing field for all.

We were mixed and moving around all day, meeting new people and engaging in innovative activities. Everyone was kind, hopeful, and just as eager to turn the feeling we were all having into a reality for everyone in their respective businesses. It felt amazing to be in a room of five hundred people all committed to serving others, creating a sense of belonging at work and embracing our differences. Imagine if we could bottle this feeling and have every employee feel this good at work. How much more effective, innovative, and profitable would we be at work? Employee engagement would rise along with morale, turnover would decrease, and all people would be commonly considered for executive positions.

Equity is closer than it has been, but we're NOT there—not by a longshot. We must continue to be diligent when choosing our workplace; we must select the right employer, one committed to hiring and promoting all people.

A critical trend occurring now is transparent pay. In several states, laws have been passed for companies to transparently disclose the pay range for each position. We must demand equal pay for the role that offers the same value, regardless of who is performing it. Korn Ferry is a top leadership development consulting firm spearheading this work with their clients, offering direction on how to create transparency and equity with compensation in business and then assess where employees are experiencing the change.

We must continue to embrace changes. No longer can we wait idly by for someone to give us a handout. We must *wake up* and create the life we've always wanted but were too afraid to choose. You're worth it! You deserve the life you desire. When doubt creeps into your mind, remember to change the narrative playing out from "I can't" to "Why Can't I?"

CONCLUSION
LIVE IT!

I am convinced we have the power to consciously change. My clients remind me daily of not only the struggles but also the courage, grace, and determination to get it right, do the hard work, and strive for positive outcomes. Regardless of the challenge, if they see a path, change is possible.

We cannot judge how anyone else manages through their own difficulty, and I support my clients by asking if their chosen course of action comes from the place of their best self, or fear. If more of us chose and act from our best selves, we will see a positive ripple effect on our lives, culture, and community.

One of my clients felt overwhelmed and undervalued by her CEO, who was purported to be a bully. This was a man of impressive height and weight who had a loud, commanding voice and used sarcasm frequently in conversation. In fact, he knew people considered him a bully.

I asked her to read an early draft of my book and spent time coaching her. Over a period of a few years, I witnessed his leadership style with her and others. I heard the stories of negative experiences he'd created by going over her head, demeaning her in front of others in meetings, and withholding information that was vital to doing her job effectively. She was exhausted and felt at her wit's end, yet something in her gut kept her there. We even talked about her defining her ideal role at her ideal company, but she continued in her job, always doing her best.

It would be easy for anyone on the outside looking at this example to determine what she "should" have done, but I heard her resolve on more than one occasion that she knew she needed to stay. In the beginning, she stayed for the people whom she helped. Every day people called her or came to her office for advice. Truly committed to helping people, she fulfilled her purpose by being present for people who were really, really struggling. At one point, an employee came to her who was giving up on life. The work and leadership struggle was too much for him to bear. She helped him through it, even calling him at home to make sure he was okay. At one point I asked her, "What about you helping yourself? What would that look like?" She felt fulfilled, however, knowing she positively impacted people daily.

Through it all, though, she kept her eye on what it would look like to have the perfect role, a role she was defining in her head and on paper. She was able to recite to me attributes of both the job and the company she would find ideal. She was committed to making a difference in a company that honored her worth and valued her as an employee. She wanted to ensure there was no glass ceiling above her, and she wanted to utilize her talents and skills in a greater scope. Through this process she defined and redefined what she wanted.

She shared with me stories of how the CEO would cut her off at the knees. He'd use sarcasm to make a point, and it was biting and hurtful to her. She frequently apologized. In one coaching session I asked her, "Why are you apologizing?"

She had to think about it for a moment. Then she said, "I guess I'm apologizing to make him feel it's okay. But it's not okay."

She had an awareness in that moment she frequently apologized, so she began to note every time she caught herself saying "I'm sorry" when it wasn't an apology. In our next session, she described how often she found herself saying this. She then made a commitment to align her thoughts and words around the goals she created for herself: for others to see her value and to work for someone who valued her. She learned to stop herself from apologizing before she uttered the words. This pattern was deeply rooted for her, and making the shift in behavior required self-reflection and awareness, to which she committed.

She started seeing changes in how people interacted with her, and she felt more empowered in the design of her life. Gradually, her work experiences started to shift. The new board solicited her help to assess the CEO, and after a long, laborious process in which she was a pivotal player, the CEO was asked to leave the company.

There were times during this extremely confidential process in which she thought she wouldn't be able to lead this charge. She had so much pressure on her with no way of expressing it to others. However, she's now in a very good position with a board that values her and what she offers. They supported her assuming a bigger role, with more responsibility and challenges, which excites her. She's eagerly looking forward to her next steps.

The contents of this book are intended to arm you with a system to achieve your goals, lead from a place of love and authenticity, and strengthen your relationships through self-love and self-awareness. The methodology is using these three steps: Define, Align, Design. Within each step is a myriad of suggestions designed to help you clearly articulate what you want and to reflect on those goals.

You can use this process for small goals. For example, imagine an exchange leads you into an argument with someone that leaves you both bothered, hurt, and wondering what to do. At that moment, define the outcome you want, and align your thoughts, words, and actions to achieve that outcome. Design as you speak with that person to settle the conflict. Remember, a course correction may be required.

The method is also ideal for big dreams and goals. The process provides the clarity of outcome and the feelings associated with achieving the goal. Follow the steps in the

Align section to ensure you're actively supporting your vision. Design what it will look like. Know that likely you'll have many course corrections along the way. Find your strength group—true friends, reading, "journaling"—to support you staying the course, and continue to build your path. Celebrate the small steps as well as the large ones.

Consider this metaphor of the application process: it's like a sprint versus a marathon. In an argument, you'll need to apply the process quickly and diligently, with continuous self-awareness and ongoing reflection until you reach the outcome. For a bigger goal, such as becoming a CEO, it's more like running a marathon. You need a steady pace, with specific mile markers laid out along the journey.

Think about all the people in businesses who move through a day with little self-reflection and awareness of their actions. Their actions or inactions have an impact on those around them. Ripple effects are created. How often do you spend reflecting on intentions, motivations, thoughts, and feelings? Look for evidence as you increase your self-reflection and awareness as it impacts others. Imagine what would happen if more people applied the three-step process of *Define, Align, Design.* Imagine the potential impact this would have within your company, relationships, and ultimately, your goals.

Use the resources to help you as you move forward. Use the book to take the Three Steps—Define, Align, Design—and the tips, tools, and guidance to develop, nurture, and bring out the best YOU. We cannot assume someone will give us a handout because we think our work will speak for itself and therefore should wait until they notice. No, we must focus on our results—the results we provide every day at work and home. It will require your commitment to the cause, and the cause is ripe. It can be hard to make this change alone. If you feel change is too hard to do by yourself, grab a friend, family member, partner, or coach to travel this new path you are creating. We will rise up, united together, have each other's backs with grace and respect and love, and receive the life we desire as well as helping others along the way.

JOURNAL

- Where can and will I use this three-step process? What goals do I want to achieve now? How will I begin? When will I begin?
- Who can I ask to hold me accountable to my dreams and my timelines?

CPSIA information can be obtained
at www.ICGtesting.com
Printed in the USA
LVHW081343221222
735718LV00014B/588

9 781734 532852